The Story of

Figure Skating

Michael Boo

BEECH TREE

New York

Permission for photographs is gratefully acknowledged: pages 2, 19, 43, 46—The World Figure Skating Museum; page 13—The Metropolitan Museum of Art, Rogers Fund, 1911 (11.92); pages 28, 54, 60, 63—*American Skating World*; pages 31, 33—20th Century Fox Film Corporation; pages 35, 89—*Ice Capades*/*American Skating World*; page 39—courtesy of Candid Productions Incorporated; pages 57, 58, 79—Margaret S. Williamson; pages 62, 110, 133—Lois Elfman/*American Skating World*; page 65—Rhonda Wiles/*American Skating World*; pages 67, 92, 105, 116, 118, 119, 124, 125, 126, 147, 153—George S. Rossano/*American Skating World*; pages 69, 72, 90, 210—David Leonardi/*American Skating World*; page 70—Mentor Management; page 73—Dawn Norman/*American Skating World*; page 77—All Sport Photographic Ltd/*American Skating World*; page 81—Diane Delozier/*American Skating World*; pages 82, 111—Nancy L. Kast/*American Skating World*; page 84—Carole Swan/*American Skating World*; page 91—Sherri Fillingham/*American Skating World*; page 95—Michael Sterling Public Relations/*American Skating World*; pages 98, 100, 107—Don Shelley/*American Skating World*; page 108—Ed Lewi/*American Skating World*; page 113—Jonathan Becker/*American Skating World*; pages 114, 167—Kolette Myers/*American Skating World*; pages 127, 128, 139, 141, 144, 149, 155, 160—Charles C. White/*American Skating World*; page 135—Shirley McLaughlin/*American Skating World*; pages 137, 158—Karen Chande/*American Skating World*; pages 142, 148, 166—Charles E. Covell/*American Skating World*; pages 146, 150, 152, 161, 187—Barb McCutcheon/*American Skating World*; page 172—Deborah J. Nelson/Satin Stitches; page 174—John M. Egbert/*American Skating World*; page 176—SP-Teri; pages 181, 183—Frank J. Zamboni & Co, Inc.; page 185—Ice Castle; page 191—Marco Entertainment

Published by Morrow Junior Books
a division of William Morrow and Company, Inc.
1350 Avenue of the Americas, New York, NY 10019
www.williammorrow.com

Printed in the United States of America.

The Library of Congress has cataloged the Morrow Junior Books edition of *The Story of Figure Skating* as follows:
Boo, Michael.
The story of figure skating / Michael Boo.
p. cm.
Includes bibliographical references and index.
Summary: Surveys the history of figure skating and examines some of its notable performers.
ISBN 0-688-15820-X
1. Skating—History—Juvenile literature. 2. Skaters—Juvenile literature.
[1. Ice skating. 2. Ice skaters.] I. Title.
GV850.4.B66 1998 796.91'2'09—dc21 98-13569 CIP AC

1 2 3 4 5 6 7 8 9 10

First Beech Tree Edition, 1998
ISBN 0-688-15821-8

To the memory of Harris Collins,
ASSOCIATE PRODUCER/DIRECTOR,
Tour of World Figure Skating Champions (now *Champions on Ice*)

Special thanks to Jana Bobek, mother of Nicole Bobek; Rosemary Brosnan, Executive Editor, Morrow Junior Books; Michele Coppola, former Associate Editor, Morrow Junior Books; Deborah J. Nelson, President, Satin Stitches; Michael Rosenberg, President, Marco Entertainment; George Spiteri, President, SP-Teri; Thomas Memorial Library (Chesterton, Indiana) research desk librarians; Donald Yontz, President, Entertainment Production Services; and Richard F. Zamboni, President, Frank J. Zamboni, Inc., & Co.

A very special thanks to Kermit Jackson, Owner and Executive Editor, *American Skating World*.

Also special thanks to my friends at *Champions on Ice*: Roger Bathurst, Wardrobe Supervisor; Tom Collins, Executive Producer; Elaine DeMore, USFSA Representative; Pat Gale, Media Coordinator; Paul Hendrickson, Production Manager; Eric Lang, Physical Therapist; Lou McClary, Security; and Sandy Reed, Coordinator.

A very special thanks to the dozens of skaters who have allowed me over the years to interview them for *American Skating World*.

CONTENTS

THIS IS A GREAT TIME IN HISTORY TO BE A FIGURE skating fan. Never before has so much skating been offered on television, giving one a chance to see a multitude of competitions, exhibitions, and theatrical productions. An increasing number of tours are traveling the world, allowing more and more fans to see their favorite skaters in person.

The dramatic increase in tours and professional competitions and exhibitions has encouraged countless well-known skaters to put off retirement, keeping them on the ice and in front of their fans well beyond the age when in previous decades they would have hung up their skates.

Skating clubs are growing, and more children and adults are discovering the joys of lacing up their boots and gliding across the ice, providing more coaches with a chance to make a living from their passion.

It wasn't so long ago that just a handful of skating programs appeared on television, with many broadcast during the holidays. A significant amount of time was dedicated to skating during the broadcast of the Winter Olympics, but the four years in between seemed like a long wait. The National and World Championships were shown without much fanfare each year, but as soon as they were over, fans had little else to look forward to.

Television viewers knew the big names from the past mainly from their memories, as former amateur champions and other professionals had little chance to stay in the spotlight. Many signed on with the glitzy and glamorous skating tours of the day. But these big-name skaters were just the icing on the cake rather than the "main event," often taking a backseat in the advertising to the costumed cartoon and fairy-tale characters. The idea of having professional competitions was a radical one. How could pros stay in shape to compete head-to-head? This seems a strange question today, now that pros are in many instances better athletes than they were as amateurs.

Today the most popular touring shows let the skating speak for itself. While some shows still feature cute animal costumes and cartoon characters, one sees the biggest reactions from the crowd at those shows where the skaters do what they do best, which is to skate with all their heart. Big names from Winter Olympics a decade earlier are still thrilling audiences with their leaps, jumps, and artistry, sometimes skating side by side with names that have just become known to the public.

This book traces the evolutions and revolutions that have occurred in figure skating over the past several decades, and even in previous centuries. It attempts to bring to life the developments, events, and personal sacrifices that have helped shape skating into one of the most popular spectator sports today.

part**One**

The Birth of Figure Skating

The First Skates

NORTHERN EUROPEANS, QUITE POSSIBLY THE VIKINGS, are credited with creating the first skates some time around the ninth century by fastening lengths of wood or bones to their everyday boots. In the Scandinavian countries, sharpened antlers also were used for blades. Archaeologists have even unearthed blades that were made from walrus teeth.

Skaters today would have an extremely difficult time skating on these ancient blades. Today's metal blades have a hollow groove running their entire length. As shallow as it is, the groove creates two very sharp edges (referred to as the inside edge and the outside edge) that grip the ice.

The earliest blades had no edges to grip the ice and help the skaters push forward, so the skaters had to carry poles. Skaters used the poles not only for balance and to keep from sliding side to side, but also, more importantly, to move forward. The poles propelled the skaters in much the same manner as those used by today's cross-country skiers.

The Dutch are credited with figuring out how to skate without poles when iron blades became available. The first all-metal skate blades showed up in Russia near the end of the 1600s. These early iron blades of the Industrial Revolution allowed skaters to use the sharpened edges to dig into the ice for propulsion.

Skates as known today did not exist centuries ago. Now, when someone mentions the word *skates,* we think of the combination of boot and blade. Back then, the word *skates* meant just the blades, which were fastened to everyday boots with straps. These straps sometimes held the blades on rather flimsily and were prone to breaking from the side-to-side stress.

Later, blades were attached to heavy and structurally weak wooden foot plates, which were then strapped on to boots. These wooden devices were an improvement over blades simply attached to the boots, but they did not absorb much stress before breaking. Leather straps would be a necessary evil until near the end of the eighteenth century, when blades began to be more solidly fastened to boots with clamps.

It wasn't until 1850 that the first modern all-steel skate was created. Philadelphia mechanic E. V. Bushnell's clip-on invention screwed a steel blade of superior hardness directly to a skate boot, eliminating the need for straps or clamps.

With Bushnell's invention, skaters could jump and spin without concern that their blades would separate from the boot. This helped make the mid-1800s a period of substantial recreational skating growth.

Gliding through Europe

In 1380, a girl named Lidwina was born in Holland (the Netherlands). Like most of her friends, she learned to skate almost as soon as she learned to walk. In 1396, she fell while skating on the ice of a frozen canal (legend has it that she was pushed over) and sustained serious internal injuries. Lidwina was bedridden the rest of her life, but before she died in 1433, she was credited with performing a variety of miracles from her bedside and is thought by many to be responsible for miracles even after her death.

Her remains were interred near her hometown of Schiedam, and in 1616 she was beatified by the Roman Catholic church, a step on the way to the sainthood that was bestowed upon her in 1890 by Pope Leo XIII. Scheidam was completely untouched by the Nazi bombing blitz that destroyed so much of Holland during World War II. Locals attribute this to the divine intervention of their hometown patron saint and enthusiastically celebrate Saint Lidwina Feast Day every April 14.

If skating were to have a patron saint, it's no surprise that she would come from the Netherlands, a country practically synonymous with the popularization of skating. The winters of northern Europe are long and cold, creating ample opportunities for skating across the ice of natural bodies of water for much of the year. That's why so many paintings of Dutch ice skating scenes are found in art museums throughout Europe, many by Dutch masters of the fourteenth through the seventeenth centuries.

Skating at Slooten, near Amsterdam, by seventeenth-century Dutch painter Jan Beerstraaten

The Dutch not only loved recreational skating, but they also used skating as an essential mode of transportation. Many villages throughout the Netherlands are connected by rivers and canals that freeze solid during the winter. During that season, long before there was such a thing as a snowplow, it often became impossible to travel the roads between countless villages. Skating became not just the preferred method of getting from one place to another—in some cases it was the only method possible.

The sport of speed skating was born when the many youngsters skating down canals and rivers began to challenge one another to races. The sport, with its extra-long blades for pushing ahead quickly, attracted throngs of cheering onlookers. Casual contests led to actual competitions, and the sport soon spread throughout the region and the nearby countries of Scandinavia. It's no wonder that of the first sixty-five Men's World Speed Skating titles, presented each year since 1893, fifty-five were won by athletes from the Netherlands and the Scandinavian countries of Norway, Sweden, and Finland.

It would take some time for skating to become popular in North America, but by the mid-1700s, the sport had crossed the North Sea. It became enough of a rage in Scotland that the world's first skating club was founded in Edinburgh in 1744.

It was not unheard of for skaters to fall through the ice of the rivers, canals, ponds, and lakes that had become natural skating venues. Mishaps like these were such a problem that when the first skating club was founded in North America in 1849, its members were required to carry ropes to rescue people who fell into frigid waters while skating. The Philadelphia Skating Club and Humane Society was so named because, in addition to skating, its members showed concern for their fellow humans by risking their lives to rescue those in danger.

Skating was enjoying the status of the "in" thing on both sides of the Atlantic.

By that time, skating was so popular in the British Isles that the cover of the very first mass-produced printed Christmas card, manufactured in London, featured a skating scene.

The Quest for Year-round Ice

Many skating enthusiasts dreamed that one day people would skate indoors, mercifully separated from icy winds and cold weather. The first recorded attempts to make artificial ice were in 1812, but it would be decades before anyone got it right. Artificial ice was produced in 1842, but it didn't prove to be solid enough for skating.

Florida inventor Dr. John Gorrie created a machine in 1850 that could make ice by using compressed air, which absorbed the heat in the water. At the time, this was not seen as a practical solution, though much later Gorrie's device laid the groundwork for more successful ice-making machines, including refrigerator ice makers.

The first covered indoor ice rink was the Skating Club House, constructed in Quebec City, Canada, in 1854. However, the ice was made naturally and kept frozen by keeping the windows open. This wasn't the significant progress that many skaters had been hoping for, but at least they could skate indoors.

In the 1860s, a system was created whereby water was flooded over metal tubes, then frozen by the tubes. A big advance came in 1865 or 1876 (history books disagree), when W. A. Parker came up with the idea of mixing brine (water saturated with salt) with carbonic acid (carbon dioxide dissolved in water), creating an artificial ice surface that was more solid and better able to withstand the rigors of skate blades than artificially frozen water alone.

British professor John Gamgee successfully created artificial ice indoors in the mid-1870s. He opened an indoor rink in Chelsea, England, that utilized a process of cooling ice by pumping glycerin and water through copper pipes and keeping the ice refrigerated with ether. The rink was microscopic by today's standards, a scant twenty-four by sixteen feet, about the size of a large residential living room. But it opened the way for larger indoor rinks.

In 1879, Gamgee's method was employed at the Glaciarium in Manchester, England. At twenty-four by forty feet, this was, at the time, the world's largest indoor ice rink.

That same year, the Wizard of Menlo Park, Thomas Alva Edison, shocked the world by inventing the incandescent lightbulb. Within the next decade, ice rinks had installed the new-fangled contraptions so that patrons could skate after dark.

Warm weather, strong winds, darkness—all the elements that had kept people off the ice at one time or another had now been conquered. Ice rinks could be enjoyed even during the summer, and warm-weather locales could now build ice rinks. Nature proved to be no match for the desires and conquests of humanity.

Why It's Called Figure Skating

While many skaters were perfectly happy just to skate around on a pond for enjoyment or to race down a canal for glory, others were starting to create the new sport and art form of figure skating. It wasn't at all like today's figure skating. The early practitioners of the discipline spent countless hours learning how to trace basic forms on the ice, mostly variations of circles and figure eights. These basic figures became known as "school figures," which is how the term *figure skating* originated.

This simple discipline evolved into something far more complex, with skaters sometimes taking hours to produce ornate and intricate figures. The most unusual of these designs became the individual calling cards of those who were best in the world, with "Can you top this?" challenges issued to others. When we look at some of these ornamental figures, it's amazing that anyone could have had enough steadiness of foot and patience to trace these complex pictures onto the ice.

An ornamental
figure

In 1772, Robert Jones wrote and published *A Treatise on Skating*, the
first comprehensive English-language textbook on figure skating.
More than a century later, in 1882, the first international skate meet
was held in Vienna, Austria. All the skaters had to demonstrate proficiency in many standardized school figures—there were more
than forty variations on the figure eight alone. In addition, the contestants were allowed to perform a figure of their own choosing and
to present a free skate routine.

In 1883, Henry Boswell, an iron worker and skater in Oxford, England, created the first skate especially made for figure skating, with a blade that resembles the one we know today. Toe picks (the notches ground into the front of every figure skate) helped the skaters stop on a dime and control their tracings and other movements.

Despite this improvement, the sport seemed to many to be more drudgery than fun. Observers noted that the faces of the figure skaters showed no joy as they immersed themselves in deep concentration to trace the intricate figures.

A century later, as school figures were being considered for elimination at the World and Olympic Championships, many were still saying that despite the self-discipline achieved through learning and perfecting school figures, tracing figures was a huge waste of skaters' time and effort, not to mention that it was something spectators could hardly care less about.

Jackson Haines: Skating's First Superstar

Jackson Haines, the father of contemporary figure skating, was born in New York City in 1840, just prior to the time of the first experiments with artificial ice. (Some books claim that he was born in Chicago.) He excelled at the tracing of figures, bringing grace and beauty to the increasingly mundane art form.

Haines was not at all thrilled by proper skating decorum, which held that skaters had to maintain a stiff, rigid posture, with arms neatly folded. He felt there had to be more to skating than tracing school figures, and he had an intense desire to liberate skating from the restrictions that had been placed upon it.

He believed that figure skating would not truly become an art form until the rules allowed for more individual self-expression. The ballet training he received in Europe and his work as a ballet instructor in Philadelphia prior to the Civil War were strong influences on Haines and allowed him to apply elements of dance to his skating.

There was no official United States Figure Skating Association National Championship until 1914, but in 1863 and 1864 Haines won the predecessor event, the Championships of America. Despite his accomplishments, he was disregarded at best and scorned at worst by fellow American skaters for being too much of a showman. He was not like the rest of them, being fond of fancy costumes and exuding a sense of grace that other skaters thought was less than appropriate.

Too radical for the established skating scene in the United States, Haines packed his bags and sailed to Europe, where he was regarded less with suspicion and more with a sense of wonder. He settled in Vienna and got to know the Strauss family of composers. The famous Johann Strauss wrote waltzes in his honor, and Haines stunned the world by doing something that is taken for granted today: He skated to music. Thomas Edison didn't invent the phonograph until 1877, so Haines employed musicians to sit by the side of the ice and perform. In the process, he taught the Viennese how to waltz on ice.

Sculpture of Jackson Haines, the father of modern figure skating, at the World Figure Skating Museum

Haines created quite a sensation in Vienna and throughout Europe. He made artistry an important element in skating and actively pursued what is now thought of as free skating. Among the moves he's credited with developing are the spiral and the spread eagle, the latter employed more than a century later to such great and memorable effect by Brian Boitano in his stunning free skate (long program) performance at the 1988 Winter Olympics.

The ever-inventive Haines also did the first sit spin, a staple in all advanced skaters' repertoires. In this move, the skater drops almost to the ice while spinning in place on one bent knee, with the other leg extended straight out or bent to the front.

Wanting to spin more freely, Haines developed a blade that was shorter than the conventional skate blade and that allowed him to do tighter turns. (The blades did not have the toe picks that Boswell would add a few years later in 1883.) He also was the first to attach a permanent blade to a boot.

He was so popular that streets were named after him in some of Europe's major cities. He was so influential that he single-handedly gave birth to the International Style of figure skating, the style we recognize and accept today as legitimate figure skating.

It seemed that there was nothing Haines couldn't do. But in 1875, in only his midthirties, he died of pneumonia in Finland while traveling by sled to a skating exhibition. An outcast in his day in his native country, he was buried in Finland under a tombstone that reads, JACKSON HAINES, IN REMEMBRANCE OF AMERICA'S SKATING KING.

The Haines Aftermath

The effect of Haines's life and work cannot be discounted. The International Style truly lived up to its name by spreading to country after country. In 1879, the first-known international skating competition was held in Stockholm, Sweden. Only men were allowed to compete, as competition was deemed "improper" for "proper" women. (Women were eventually allowed into international competitions, but for the sake of modesty they had to wear long dresses that practically touched the ice.)

That same year saw the creation of the world's first organized skating governing body, the National Skating Association of Great Britain. Although speed skaters were the only original members, the organization was eventually opened to the vast number of figure skaters caught up in the craze kindled by Haines's success.

The year 1879 was an active one for the evolution of figure skating, for in addition to the two events just mentioned, the year also saw the first skating carnival take place on manufactured ice. Carnivals were nothing new, with masked skaters in ornate costumes skating about as spectators watched from rinkside seats. But this carnival took place on a large, mechanically frozen surface in New York City's Madison Square Garden, and, as such, it attracted quite a bit of media attention.

Ironically, word of Haines's success began to filter back to the United States, and American skaters started to adopt his more musical and expressive style as their own. Numerous new skating clubs were formed in the country that had at one time seemed to discard him.

As a result, Louis Rubenstein, a Canadian International Style disciple and twelve-time Canadian National Champion, saw a need for the clubs to unite in common purpose. He helped found not only the Amateur Figure Skating Association of Canada in 1878 (which later became the Canadian Figure Skating Association) but also the International Skating Union of America and the National Amateur Skating Association of the United States—organizations comprising many new and previously existing skating clubs.

In 1884, Norwegian all-around skater Axel Paulsen visited North America. (He was an "all-around" skater because he excelled as both a speed skater and a figure skater.) He managed to win indoor track races and long-distance events of ten and twenty-five miles by skating with his arms positioned behind his back over long distances and being more aerodynamic than anyone else.

Paulsen also presented figure skating demonstrations in the International Style and amazed all with his signature jump, for which he leaped into the air forward, rotated one-and-a-half revolutions in the air, and then landed backward on the opposite foot. The jump, known as the axel, is today a staple in every competitive skater's arsenal of tricks, with more advanced skaters pulling off double axels and triple axels, the latter the most difficult of all triple jumps. Despite being a single jump, Paulsen's axel was the most challenging jump yet seen in its day.

In addition to fostering goodwill and camaraderie among figure skaters, organizations such as the United States Figure Skating Association became clearinghouses for the standardization of competitions and proficiency tests. These encourage the use of proper techniques and help skaters move up the competitive ladder.

The International Skating Union (ISU) was formed in 1892, lending its approval to the first World Figure Skating Championships in St. Petersburg, Russia, in 1896, which were won by Gilbert Fuchs, a German. (Ladies' and Pairs events had yet to break onto the internationally judged skating scene, and it would be a long time before Ice Dancing became recognized.)

By the end of the nineteenth century, children all around the world were reading a book by Mary Mapes Dodge that was written in 1885. The main character of the book is a young boy skater growing up in Holland, a country that Dodge described in stunning and picturesque detail despite never having been there. More than a century later, *Hans Brinker and the Silver Skates* remains the most popular book ever written about skating.

Skating Becomes a Spectator Sport

Welcome, Ladies

THE TURN OF THE TWENTIETH CENTURY WAS A TIME of great hope and expectations. Edison's lightbulb, no longer an oddity in homes and workplaces, was changing the way that people lived. Early automobiles were rolling out of factories, changing the way people traveled. Inventors Wilbur and Orville Wright made the first airplane flight in Kitty Hawk, North Carolina, in 1903, giving people a glimpse of commercial transportation in the future. For the most part, the world was at peace.

It was a time of great growth for recreation and for competitive figure skating.

In 1901, Sweden's Ulrich Salchow, creator of the jump that bears his last name and eventual President of the International Skating Union (ISU), won the first of his ten ISU World Figure Skating Championships between that year and 1911, his string of victories interrupted only in 1906. In 1902, he was almost defeated by Great Britain's Madge Syers, the only time men and women ever competed head-to-head at the World Championships.

As one might imagine, a woman's earning the silver medal in singles skating at the most prestigious skating event in the world caused quite a stir. The truth is, no one had seen this as a potential problem, because no one among the rule makers thought that a woman might be that good in a "man's sport," and Syers was the first woman ever to apply to compete in the World Championships.

After Syers's near upset of Salchow—and some sports observers thought she should have won—the rules were changed, and women had to wait until 1906 to compete for the World Championship in their own division. Naturally, the gold medalist of the first two

Ladies' World Championships was none other than Madge Syers.

It's not inconceivable that Syers might have toppled Salchow in 1902 had she spent more of her time as a singles skater. Amazingly, she was also one of the top Pairs in the world, a fact that would have to wait until 1908 to be proven.

The Ladies contestants, once they were formally allowed to compete, had to wear long dresses that came down to the top of their skates to preserve their modesty. "Real" ladies didn't expose their ankles in public. (To this day, women are officially known as Ladies in the language of the ISU.)

It's not known what the women skaters thought of skating's Victorian mind-set. A half century earlier, a German woman was stoned to death for skating, despite the fact that women had been skating in neighboring Holland for centuries.

Whatever the reason, perhaps some of the women skaters who entered the first World and Olympic Championships considered long dresses a small price to pay for being on the ice.

The Era of Summer "Winter" Olympics

The first modern-day Olympics were held in Athens, Greece, in 1896. The ISU had attempted to get figure skating into the schedule but was turned down by the International Olympic Committee (IOC). However, the IOC relented, and in 1908 figure skating was allowed in the Olympics, the only winter sport to be included in the summer games in London, England.

There was a practical reason why skating was the only winter sport to be allowed in the Olympics. There was no separate Winter Olympics until 1924 in Chamonix, France. Artificial ice surfaces for summer skating were not unusual by 1908, but artificial snow for ski jumps and cross-country ski trails was not yet common. And besides, the English had perfected artificial ice and were able to offer a venue that thumbed its nose at the heat of summer.

As expected, Ulrich Salchow won the 1908 Olympic Men's gold

medal, leading the Swedish men to a gold, silver, and bronze medal sweep of the Olympics. Men from Sweden and Austria won every one of the first six Olympic titles in figure skating (1908, 1920, 1924, 1928, 1932, and 1936). Ladies from Great Britain, Sweden, Austria, and Norway and Pairs from Germany, Finland, Austria, and France did the same.

More dramatically, men from Germany, Austria, and Sweden won every one of the first thirty-six World titles (through 1936, with a few years missing during World War I). Up through the same year, Ladies' skaters from Great Britain, Hungary, Austria, and Norway won every one of the first twenty-four World titles. Over that same time frame, Pairs champions came only from Germany, Great Britain, Finland, Austria, France, and Hungary.

What's the point? At least part of every one of those European countries has long winters. Throughout the world, there were still relatively few indoor rinks. Therefore, skaters from the more frigid countries had an advantage. It's also important to note that skaters didn't train with coaches in other countries to the extent that they do now. The best-trained skaters in those days came from cold climates with ample natural ice, just as the best-trained surfers today come from warm climates with ample waves.

But back to the 1908 Olympics: The unsinkable Madge Syers was still in good enough form after nearly upsetting Salchow at Worlds six years earlier to follow her 1906 and 1907 World titles with the first Olympic gold medal presented to a Ladies' Champion.

The Pairs skaters of the 1800s and early 1900s did not do lifts and throws, as they do today. Remember that the women had to wear long dresses, and landing on the dress after an aerial maneuver would have been disastrous. Instead, the Pairs glided around the ice in close contact with each other. If you were to see such a routine today, you would be forgiven for mistaking it for early Ice Dancing.

Anna Hubler and Heinrich Burger of Germany won the 1908 Olympic Pairs title, along with the first-ever World Pairs title the same year and another World Championship two years later. However, the real story in Pairs may have been, once again, Madge Syers. With her husband, Edgar, she captured the Olympic bronze medal in Pairs. She was truly a versatile athlete.

There was no figure skating at the Stockholm, Sweden, Summer Games in 1912, as no satisfactory artificial rink existed in the city, so there was a twelve-year gap between Olympic figure skating titles. (No Olympics were held in 1916 during World War I.)

There would be one more Olympics in which figure skating was a medal event during the Summer Games. The Belgian Summer Games of 1920 in Antwerp saw Sweden's Gillis Grafstrom win the first of his three Olympic gold medals; he won the others in 1924 and 1928. Salchow placed just out of the medals in fourth place, skating on an injured leg, nine years after the last of his ten World Championships and at the "advanced" age of forty-two.

Grafstrom astounded audiences by performing the first "flying" sit spin, a sit spin approached directly from a jump. But over the extensive period of his three Olympics victories, and despite adding many new jumps and spins to his skating repertoire, he won only three World titles—in 1922, 1924, and 1929. We'll never know if Grafstrom could have won additional World gold medals, as there were no ISU World Championships from 1915 through 1921, while the world was at war. Instead of skating against one another, athletes were shooting at one another.

Charlotte: Skating's First Ice Queen

On May 7, 1915, the German military sank the *Lusitania*, an English luxury liner, resulting in a great loss of civilian life. This act of aggression prompted the United States to declare war on Germany. Despite that, one of the most beloved entertainers in America was a German girl who was brought to America the same year the *Lusitania* went down.

Charlotte Oelschlagel was spotted in a Berlin nightclub by Charles

Dillingham, who was in Europe looking for talent to play at his New York City theater, the massive six-thousand-seat Hippodrome. As the Hippodrome was the largest theater in the world, Dillingham wasn't looking for just *any* act—he needed to find real star quality, and he found it in seventeen-year-old Charlotte. The entertainer (who never used her last name professionally) was packing the crowds in for *Charlotte's Ice Revue,* a glitzy ice show with a supporting cast of sixty-five skaters that had been playing the German capital for the previous two years.

Charlotte was the talk of Berlin and very soon, she and her entire cast were the talk of Broadway. Dillingham took a chance that America's first large-scale ice show would be a success, signing the entire entourage to a six-week deal and changing the name of the show to *Flirting in St. Moritz.* His gamble was richly rewarded, as Charlotte's supreme artistry and the show's remarkable staying power filled the massive Hippodrome every day (sometimes twice daily) for three years.

It is said that Charlotte inspired hotels and resorts throughout the eastern United States to build indoor ice rinks for ice shows of their own and that she was the first woman to perform an axel jump. Little girls begged for Charlotte dolls. Popular songs were written about the star. She was a one-person cottage industry—skating's first queen of the ice. Though she never had a World or Olympic skating medal to her name, she created a move with her future husband that all World and Olympic Pairs must now perform if they have any hopes of success—the death spiral. This is the dramatic spin in which the female rotates on one skate around her male partner with the back of her head almost touching the ice. (Some historians state that the first death spiral was performed many years later by Canadian Pairs team Suzanne Morrow and Wallace Diestelmeyer, World bronze medalists in 1948, while others simply state that the pair was the first to do a death spiral in international competition.)

Charlotte also created the "Charlotte Stop," in which she would

glide on one leg, pivoting forward from the waist, and suddenly stop as if she had magical brakes. It's a move that many skaters have exploited since.

Charlotte became skating's first movie star, appearing in the 1916 silent film *The Frozen Warning.* The film, the first skating motion picture to be made, was split into six parts, intended to be viewed in installments, like so many of the "continuing adventure" serials that were popular in the movie houses of the day.

In the film, an up-to-no-good secret agent from a sinister foreign government steals a powerful new weapon from Charlotte's on-screen inventor boyfriend. She learns about the event and attempts to turn the tables on the secret agent during a skating performance. Now this is where things get really good: During her performance, she traces the word *spies* on the ice with her skates and then leaps into the air, pointing toward the villain. The spy is caught, the weapon is recovered, and Charlotte is honored for her courageous heroism. You have to love it.

Sonja Henie: One in a Million

For the most part, the 1920s were years of prosperity throughout the industrialized world. World War I was over, and the Great Depression wouldn't strike until October 1929.

Out of an earlier organization, the United States Figure Skating Association (USFSA) was founded in 1921, with only seven skating clubs as charter members. (Today, there are more than 450 member clubs throughout the United States.) The USFSA immediately joined the ISU and two years later published the first edition of *Skating*, the body's official magazine, which is still published today.

The first true Winter Olympics (in Chamonix, France, in 1924) are remembered less for who won (Grafstrom, among others, with his second Olympic Men's gold) than for those who didn't. The French Pairs team of Andrée Joly and Pierre Brunet took the bronze medal but came back in 1928 and 1932 to win two Olympic Pairs

Charlotte, the German youngster who became skating's first ice queen, demonstrating a dramatic stag leap

gold medals with their trailblazing use of dramatic, gravity-defying lifts. They also had a curious habit of winning the World Championship in alternate years: 1926, 1928, 1930, and 1932.

Pairs skaters had just started to develop movements where they would skate apart from each other, but they were still doing similar movements. The lifts Joly and Brunet were fond of meant that each of the Pairs skaters would undertake a unique and individual role in the partnership. This was radical for its day.

Even though Joly and Brunet didn't win the big one in 1924, at least they got a medal. An eleven-year-old girl who entered the Ladies' competition placed dead last (in thirteenth place) at her first Olympics—although she would someday change the world of figure skating forever.

Sonja Henie was an expert at tracing figures and an advocate of combining ballet with figure skating. She was Norwegian National Champion at the tender age of ten, but she was a bit ahead of her time for international tastes at the 1924 Winter Olympics, wearing white dresses instead of the traditional black. Worse yet, in the eyes of the judges, she wore short dresses so she would have the freedom necessary to jump.

Just three years later, in Oslo, Norway, fourteen-year-old Henie would win the first of her ten consecutive World titles. And four years after her less-than-illustrious Olympic debut, she won the first of her three Olympic singles titles in St. Moritz, Switzerland, also winning Olympic gold in 1932 (in Lake Placid, New York—the first Olympics to be held in North America) and 1936. (The only other skater who has as many World and Olympic titles is Pairs Champion Irina Rodnina, who won her ten World and three Olympic titles with two different partners from 1969 through 1980.)

Three-time Olympic gold medalist Sonja Henie

In between her second and third Olympic gold medals, Henie performed in a 1934 show at the Berlin Ice Palace and was photographed shaking hands with Nazi leader Adolf Hitler. The photo would come back to haunt her years later.

Henie was simply so powerful and athletic, graceful, and artistic that the judges had little choice but to recognize that the world of Ladies' skating was changing right in front of their eyes. She introduced elements of dance into her free skate programs and had more of an impact on the public than even Charlotte did.

Meanwhile, Henie's path crossed that of Chicago sports promoter Arthur M. Wirtz, although neither realized just how important each was to become to the other. Wirtz was famous for his financial interests in a number of sports arenas and teams, and in 1935 he produced a two-night ice show at his cavernous Chicago Stadium. He didn't spend much money to produce it, but he made a financial killing from its commercial success.

Less than two weeks after her 1936 Olympic victory, Henie retired from amateur competition and signed a contract with Wirtz, creating a partnership that lasted fifteen years. During that time, Henie and her *Hollywood Ice Revue* became the biggest single attraction ever to hit arenas in North America, breaking box office records everywhere she went.

In 1937, the first of Henie's eleven movies was released. *One in a Million* broke box office records of its own. When she felt uncomfortable playing a romantic scene in a later movie with Tyrone Power, she suggested that maybe she would feel more at ease if she put on her skates.

In 1940, she teamed up with Wirtz to co-produce *It Happens on Ice* at the Center Theatre in New York City's Rockefeller Center. For ten years, the Center was the only venue in America that featured nothing but ice shows. Although she was just co-producer and not the star of the show, *It Happens on Ice* set attendance records for a Broadway production.

Henie became a U.S. citizen in 1941 and was one of the wealthiest entertainers of her day. The *One in a Million* woman became the first female athlete to become a millionaire. During World War II, she was approached by her fellow Norwegians to contribute finan-

The Famous *Hawaiian Dance*

All of the several special numbers Sonja Henie has created for performance before the American public have been acclaimed, but most popular of all is her famous interpretation of the Hula.

Here the coordination of hands and feet is at its perfect best. Miss Henie devoted much time to the study of hand movements with the greatest Hawaiian dancers, whose genius at telling a story with their hands and fingers is without equal anywhere.

As a result, Miss Henie's Hawaiian Dance is completely authentic, and has the added charm of her rhythmic expertness on skates.

The Hawaiian Dance is being included in the 1947 "Hollywood Ice Revue" because audiences which have seen it before simply wouldn't listen to having it omitted. Besides, it is one of Miss Henie's favorite numbers.

The glamorous Hawaiian dance dress was just one of the many extravagant costumes Sonja Henie wore during the 1947 *Hollywood Ice Revue.*

cially to the Norwegian resistance movement that was fighting the Nazis. She turned them down by stating that she was an American now, and many never forgave her. In addition, they remembered the story about the photo of her with Hitler.

When Nazi troops advanced through Norway, she received a phone call that the troops were closing in on her residence. She instructed that the photo be put on prominent display in the house. When the troops entered the house and saw the photo of Henie with Hitler, they instantly refused to loot her home.

In 1968, she tried to make amends for not helping out her native country during World War II by donating her vast collection of modern art to a public museum she established with her husband near Oslo.

In 1951, Henie parted ways with Wirtz and formed the *Sonja Henie Ice Revue*. While not as successful as the earlier efforts with Wirtz, this tour changed the face of skating by introducing the Zamboni Ice Resurfacer to the world. Before Henie's tour, only one other Zamboni existed—at the ice rink built and managed by inventor Frank Zamboni. Zamboni custom-built a second machine at Henie's request, and everywhere the tour went, rink managers decided they had to have a Zamboni for themselves.

Three years later, she skated in Oslo with *Holiday on Ice*. Over thirty-three days, more people came out to see her skate than resided in Norway's capital city.

Early Ice Extravaganzas

In a repeat of what happened during World War I, there were no World Championships or Winter Olympics during the tumultuous years of World War II. The war eliminated Worlds from 1940 through 1946 and the 1940 and 1944 Olympics.

In 1936, America's first outdoor artificial ice rink opened in the plaza of New York City's Rockefeller Center. It still remains open each winter, and thousands of people gather every week to glide around on the public ice.

Also in 1936 (which was the same year Henie's *Hollywood Ice Revue* took to the road), Shipstads and Johnson *Ice Follies* was founded as the world's first large-scale traveling ice show, breaking attendance records throughout the United States and Canada. Although it was "large-scale," the effects of the Depression meant that the promoters could hire only a couple of dozen skaters at first. This show provided retired amateurs with an opportunity to keep skating past their competitive years, more often than not as members of the chorus line.

Ice Capades brought the flamboyant style and unabashed glitz of a Las Vegas floor show to hundreds of cities throughout the world.

In 1940, *Ice Capades* debuted, bringing movies, books, operas, and other cultural diversions to the ice, and it is largely credited with giving wide exposure to Ice Dancing, which wasn't to become a World Championship sport until 1952 and an Olympic sport until 1976. *Ice Capades* performed a completely new show each year. The operation eventually expanded to three separate touring companies for a period of several years, but through the 1980s and '90s it experienced numerous financial problems and had a number of owners (including Olympic gold medalist Dorothy Hamill).

Holiday on Ice was formed in 1944 and became known for bringing ice spectacles to locales that would otherwise never have had a chance to host one, such as Mexico, Cuba, Central and South America, and the Caribbean islands of the West Indies. The operation traveled with its own refrigeration equipment and could make its own 100- by 60-foot portable ice rink wherever it went.

Eventually, before the production ceased operations, *Holiday on Ice* skaters performed on every continent except Antarctica. In 1959, they became the first ice show to play behind the Iron Curtain, at a time when relationships between the United States and the then–Soviet Union were rather strained. About one million Muscovites saw the production over a two-month run.

Holiday on Ice became *Walt Disney's World on Ice* in 1981 and since then has directed its marketing appeal to children, often focusing on bringing Disney films to life.

Each of the three big ice companies was famous for producing lavish, sometimes garish and "over the top," always spectacular and fabulously costumed production numbers. They brought the flamboyance of a circus troupe to life on the ice. The big-budget productions overwhelmed the senses with visually explosive color, costumes, and pageantry. The operative word seemed to be MORE! The souls of these shows live on today in the grandiose, skimpy-on-costumes-but-big-on-feather-headdresses showgirl productions seen in Las Vegas.

The Early TV Days

The World War II Vacuum

THE HISTORY OF TWENTIETH-CENTURY FIGURE skating in the United States is generally thought of as being either pre-1961 or post-1961, for reasons that will later be discussed. And as for the pre-1961 days, they can be thought of as being pre–Sonja Henie and post–Sonja Henie, so much did she influence the sport and the way it was marketed.

Henie's popularity inspired many skaters to take to the ice. However, the effect of her retirement in 1936 from amateur competition was soon muted by the brewing storm clouds of World War II. Had Henie stayed eligible for amateur competition, she would not have been able to defend her title at the 1940 Winter Olympics. There were none.

In 1936, Nazi Germany staged the Winter Olympics in Garmisch. If the world had known then what it would find out a few years later when the crimes of the Holocaust came to light, there might not have been the 1936 Winter Olympics either. It's ironic that the country that staged the last Winter Olympics prior to World War II would be most responsible for the cancellation of the Winter Olympics in 1940. Germany gave the world no choice, after they invaded Poland in 1939.

Nor were there Winter Olympics in 1944. Also affected by the war were the World Championships, which were canceled for seven years, from 1940 through 1946. There's no telling whose might have been a household name yet today had there been no war.

Many skaters were certainly in their prime during those years, but without a world stage to shine on, those who were not still in their prime when the war was over faded into obscurity. Some probably wanted to compete in top form after the war, but by then time just wasn't on their side.

The Postwar Years and Dick Button

One skater who might have made a greater impact had there been no World War II was Canada's Barbara Ann Scott, Canadian Ladies' Champion in 1944, 1945, 1946, and 1948. In 1947 and 1948, Scott won the ISU's World Ladies' Championship, and she was victorious as well at the 1948 Winter Olympics in St. Moritz, Switzerland. Her 1947 World victory made her the first North American to win an ISU World Championship.

The year of Scott's second World Championship saw other Canadian skaters garner attention as well. Pairs team Suzanne Morrow and Wallace Diestelmeyer is credited with doing the first death spiral at a World Championship, during a performance that earned them the bronze medal.

The Soviets, who would virtually own the World and Olympics Pairs titles from 1964 on and the Ice Dancing titles from 1970 on (Ice Dancing wasn't an Olympic event until 1976), were unknown on the world stage after World War II. In fact, the only Russian/Soviet Pairs medal earned at the World Championships prior to 1962 was a single bronze, won by the Russian team of A. L. Fischer and L. P. Popowa at the 1908 World Championships, the first at which a Pairs competition was held.

In 1946, the world got its first glimpses of a man known by skating fans today as a popular and beloved television skating commentator and a producer of professional skating competitions. That year, Richard "Dick" Button started compiling an impressive string of U.S. Men's gold medal victories, winning the first Men's National Championship to be decided since 1943. This propelled him to prominence as the top male skater in the country as soon as the war was over. He stayed in that position for seven straight years, from 1946 through 1952. He also won five straight World Championships

Dick Button defies gravity during a stunning Russian split.

(1948 through 1952) and won the Men's gold medal at both the 1948 and 1952 Winter Olympics.

His 1948 Olympic victory at the age of eighteen makes him the youngest man ever to win an Olympics singles championship. In addition, it gave the United States its first-ever Olympic skating gold medal in any of the skating disciplines and its first-ever Olympic Men's medal of any color.

Button's 1946 National Championship came just four years after he took his first skating lesson. He was driven to succeed at introducing increasingly more difficult jumps into competitions. At the 1952 Winter Olympics, he became the first skater successfully to perform any triple jump, in this case a triple loop. He was never satisfied with playing it safe, and as he introduced new jumps, other skaters found it harder and harder to keep up with his lead.

Even today, it's amazing to read the list of Dick Button firsts. (Remember that only people who succeed at accomplishing a jump in competition go into the record books. Practices don't count. Lots of almost-firsts have happened in practices.)

In 1945, Button performed the first double salchow, soon adding the double loop and double lutz to his repertoire of jumps. At the 1948 Winter Olympics, he nailed the first two-and-a-half-rotation jump in history, the double axel.

Consider that Axel Paulsen first performed the single axel in 1882, and that wasn't even in a formal competition. It would take sixty-six years before someone was able to stretch an axel out to a double. It would take someone else another thirty years to pull off a triple axel—Canada's Vern Taylor at the 1978 World Championships.

But for all of Button's accomplishments, it was his performance of the first triple loop in 1952 that is most talked about. Today, even junior-level skaters attempt triple loops, the easiest of all triple jumps. But in 1952, Dick Button had no one who could tell him, based on his or her own experience, how it could be done.

American Singles Dominate

The same year of Button's landmark triple, Ice Dancing became a part of the World Championships. Jean Westwood and Lawrence Demmy of Great Britain won the first title and repeated the victory each of the next three years. Three different British Ice Dancing teams would win the next five Worlds (1956 through 1960), and Diane Towler and Bernard Ford would win four more in a row for Great Britain from 1966 through 1969.

In 1950, Karol and Peter Kennedy became the first Americans to win the Pairs World Championship. Ten different Pairs teams won the World Championships from 1947 through 1964. Only one Pairs team seemed to have a lock on the World Championships leading up to Winter Olympics during that same period. Canada's Barbara Wagner and Robert Paul won four Worlds in a row (1957 through 1960) and took gold at the 1960 Winter Olympics.

During the post-Button years, the Men's and Ladies' scene on the world stage was firmly in America's control.

Two brothers would take over the mantle from Button once he retired from amateur competition. Together, with Button, they gave the United States a streak of twelve consecutive Men's World Championships and four consecutive Olympic Men's gold medals. Hayes Alan Jenkins won the 1953, 1954, 1955, and 1956 Worlds and the 1956 Winter Olympics. David Jenkins picked up from his older sibling, winning the 1957, 1958, and 1959 World Championships and the 1960 Winter Olympics. Between the two of them, they also won eight consecutive USFSA Championships, four each, from 1953 through 1960. Skating was a way of life in the Jenkins family. Their sister was an accomplished skater, and their mother served as a USFSA judge.

Tenley Albright won the USFSA Ladies' Championship in 1952, the year she took the silver medal at the Winter Olympics. She recaptured her USFSA crown each of the next four years. In 1953, she became the first American woman to win the World Championship, and repeated as World Champion in 1955, capping off her competitive career with a gold medal performance at the 1956 Winter Olympics in Cortina, Italy.

The year of her Olympic victory was an interesting one in the annals of U.S. Ladies' Champions, for although Albright defeated silver medalist Carol Heiss for the fourth year in a row at the USFSA Championship and would go on to win the Olympics over second-place Heiss, her World team comrade would turn the tables one month after the Olympics by forcing Albright to settle for the silver medal at the 1956 World Championships.

Albright certainly had a bright amateur career, and there is little doubt that she would have had a successful professional career as well, if she had so chosen. However, Albright had other plans. She had wanted to be a doctor for several years and saw skating as a means of accomplishing her higher goal. She had seen her share of doctors as a youth, having been stricken with childhood polio. Many victims of this now virtually unheard-of disease never walked again. Albright fought it and skated to build up her strength step-by-step, eventually becoming a World and Olympic Champion. And after attaining her goal of being the best skater in the world, she completed college, went on to medical school, and became a highly respected surgeon.

Albright never relinquished her amateur status. Remarkably, she remains the only Olympic singles gold medalist, man or woman, since 1928, who did not turn pro.

Carol Heiss first appeared on the world stage in 1953, as silver medalist behind Albright at the USFSA Championship and as fourth-place finisher in that year's World Championship. She was only thirteen years old. In the early 1920s, Sonja Henie had been the first Ladies' skater to do a single axel jump. Heiss became the first to do

World and
Olympic
Champion
Carol Heiss

a double axel. As for placing behind Albright at Nationals, finishing second to her teammate would be something she would have to get used to.

During the last four years (1953 through 1956) of Albright's five-year USFSA winning streak, Heiss had to settle for the silver medal at Nationals and wait her turn for the gold. Patience paid off, and Heiss won four consecutive USFSA and World Championship gold medals in the years immediately afterward, in addition to her upset victory over newly crowned Olympic Champion Albright in 1956 when Heiss was sixteen years old. Today, a sixteen-year-old Ladies' World Champion would not be unusual. When Heiss won her first Worlds in 1956, only Sonja Henie had been younger when she won her first Worlds.

The payoff came in 1960, when Heiss won the Winter Olympics Ladies' gold medal in Squaw Valley, California. But the big news was yet to come, presented at the World Championships just after the Olympics. After winning another Worlds title, she announced her engagement to U.S. World and Olympic Men's Champion Hayes Alan Jenkins. Jenkins became perhaps the man most surrounded by skating family: his mother, sister, brother, and now his wife.

Perhaps partially because of the successes enjoyed by U.S. skaters on the world level, ice arenas started popping up around the country. In 1943, there were only about one hundred rinks in the entire nation. About that same number were added in 1958 alone. That year, Mary Mapes Dodge's 1885 classic novel, *Hans Brinker and the Silver Skates*, was made into a feature-length production by NBC-TV, supposedly the first time that a dramatic television production employed figure skaters.

Interest in skating was at a record high in the United States. Rinks were being built; skating features were being made for television; American touring companies were heading behind the Iron Curtain. American skaters were the dominant force in singles skating. The 1960 Winter Olympics made it two Winter Games in a row that

American singles skaters would take the gold medals, and the third that Men would do so—Button in 1952, Hayes Alan Jenkins and Albright in 1956, and David Jenkins and Heiss in 1960.

It was the best of times for American figure skating. But suddenly, it was the worst of times.

Long Live the Dream: Team USA—1961

In 1961, the world came crashing down around American figure skating.

The big names had turned pro after the 1960 Olympics and World Championships. That allowed a new generation of American skaters to move up the ranks and take the mantle of being best in the country.

The 1961 USFSA Nationals were held in late January in Colorado Springs, Colorado. There were many new faces on the medals stand, names that everyone expected would soon be world famous.

Winning the USFSA Men's Championship was Bradley Lord, who had never before stood on the U.S. Championship medals podium. Winning the Ladies' title was Laurence Owen, whose highest placement at Nationals had been a bronze medal in 1960. Maribel Owen (sister to Laurence) and Dudley Richards won Pairs gold after finishing second the year before. The 1961 USFSA National Ice Dance Championship was won by Dianne Sherbloom and Larry Pierce.

Less than a month after the National Championships, on Tuesday, February 14, the entire U.S. World Team of eighteen skaters—plus sixteen coaches, USFSA officials, family members, and friends—regrouped at New York's Idlewild Airport (now known as Kennedy International).

It was a joyous day, not just because all looked forward to the upcoming World Championships in Prague, Czechoslovakia, but also because it was Valentine's Day.

All boarded the plane and headed off across the Atlantic Ocean in an attempt to bring home more World gold medals. After the reign

of Button, the Jenkins brothers, Albright, and Heiss, the nation's skating fans had come to expect nothing less.

The Boeing 707, carrying seventy-four people, came in for a refueling stop in Brussels, Belgium, the morning of February 15. Close to landing, the plane's landing gear was raised by the pilot, without explanation to the control tower. As the plane pulled out of its landing pattern and started to climb, it began to shake violently and make unusual loud noises. Flight 548 then fell to earth. All aboard were killed. The hopes of a nation were shattered, and skating fans around the world went into mourning.

There can be no argument that February 15, 1961, was the worst day in the history of figure skating.

Stunned by the tragedy, the ISU canceled the World Championships. It would have been unthinkable to continue.

Since 1961, the USFSA's Memorial Fund has served as a living memorial to those who were lost that tragic day. The fund is financed through voluntary contributions from fans, skate clubs, and other organizations, not-for-profit foundations, and corporations. Each year, hundreds of skaters receive financial assistance from the Memorial Fund so that they may continue their training and education.

But even though the memory lives on, a part of the soul and heart of every skating fan perished along with the 1961 U.S. World Team. February 15, 1961, is the day the dream died.

The United States figure skating team and its coaches posing in front of the plane that was to crash—with no survivors—on the way to the 1961 World Championships

part **Two**

The Age of Artistry

American Skating Rebounds

AFTER THE 1961 PLANE CRASH, MANY OBSERVERS predicted that it would be more than a decade before the American competitive skating scene would be back to something that resembled normal. The loss of three of the country's top coaches meant there was a serious lack of coaching talent to train the top skaters of America's cloudy skating future. Italy's Carlo Fassi and other coaches from Europe suddenly found themselves in demand on the North American side of the Atlantic Ocean.

The 1962 U.S. National Championships were held in Boston, Massachusetts. Competing for top honors were a large number of essentially unknown skaters. Monty Hoyt won the Men's Championship, placed third in 1963 and 1964, and then disappeared from the news. Barbara Roles—U.S. bronze medalist in 1959 and silver medalist in 1960 and 1960 World bronze medalist—won the Ladies' Championship, her life having been spared because she wasn't on the podium at the 1961 Nationals. She went on to have a long career in shows and in coaching. Dorotheyann Nelson and Pieter Kollen won Pairs, and Yvonne Littlefield and Peter Betts won Ice Dancing honors.

The 1962 World Championships were held in Prague, Czechoslovakia, the city that was to have hosted the canceled event in 1961. It had to be eerie for the American team to travel to that location and skate in the very arena that was to have been witness to the skating efforts of so many deceased American skaters. As expected, no Americans won medals, the skaters having been forced to carry the mantle of their country years earlier than originally expected. It would be 1965 before an American singles skater, Pairs, or Ice Dancing team would again ascend to the World Championships podium.

A highlight of the 1962 Worlds was Canada's Don Jackson pulling off the first triple lutz jump ever performed in competition, to win the Men's title.

Tragedy struck the world of figure skating once again on Halloween in 1963. A butane tank exploded at the Indianapolis (Indiana) Fairgrounds Coliseum, collapsing part of the building and killing seventy-five and injuring hundreds of skating fans who had come out to see a performance of *Holiday on Ice*.

The years 1963 and 1964 saw no U.S. skaters on the World Championships podium. The drought of American skaters, though expected, was a bit hard for some to accept. There had been at least one American singles on the podium every year from 1947 through 1960, including twenty-six Men's and seventeen Ladies' medals, and six World medals each for U.S. Pairs and Ice Dancing teams.

Though the U.S. Pairs team of Vivian and Ronald Joseph was awarded the bronze medal at the 1964 Winter Olympics, the pair did not have the honor of standing on the medals podium in Innsbruck, Austria. The team of Marika Kilius and Hans Baumler from the Federal Republic of Germany (West Germany) had signed a contract to appear in an ice show before they competed in the Olympics. When this was proven, they had to forfeit their silver medal, moving the bronze medal team up to silver and the fourth-place team of Joseph and Joseph up to bronze. Today, things have totally changed. One might be forgiven for wondering if skaters could be disqualified for *not* having a pro contract in hand before the Olympics.

At the 1965 Worlds, Canada's Petra Burka became the first woman to perform a triple jump (a salchow) in Ladies' World Championship competition.

Slowly, the World Championship medals tide started to turn. Ice Dancers Lorna Dyer and John Carrell captured the World bronze in 1965 and 1966 and took silver in 1967. That year, they were stopped from winning the gold by Great Britain's four-time (1966–1969) World Champions team of Diane Towler and Bernard Ford, the same team that had stopped U.S. team Kristin Fortune and Dennis Sveum in 1966. Ice Dancers Judy Schwomeyer and James Sladky took the bronze in 1969 and the silver in 1970, stopped only by the Soviet Union's Liudmila Pakhomova and Aleksandr Gorshkov, who won the first of their six World golds.

Pairs wouldn't see a U.S. team on the Worlds podium until 1966, when Cynthia and Ronald Kauffman won their first of three straight World bronze medals. Scott Allen captured the Men's silver medal at Worlds in 1965, and Gary Visconti took the bronze in 1966 and 1967. Tim Wood captured silver in 1968 and won the title in 1969 and 1970. But it was in the Ladies' competition that the United States would find the first post-crash, media-savvy, business-whiz, big-smile, everybody-loves-'em banner carrier.

American Sweethearts: Fleming and Lynn

Peggy Fleming was twelve years old when her coach was killed in the 1961 plane crash. She then went to Colorado Springs to study with the Italian coach Carlo Fassi. In 1964, Fleming won the first of five consecutive U.S. Championships. She was sixth at the 1964 Winter Olympics in Innsbruck, Austria, and popped onto the Worlds medal podium with a bronze in 1965. In 1966, 1967, and 1968, she won the World Championship and struck pay dirt by winning the 1968 Winter Olympics in Grenoble, France—the first Winter Olympics to be broadcast worldwide.

Around the world, millions marveled at Fleming's ability to float gently across the ice, seemingly without effort. At nineteen, she was, for the time, the third youngest Ladies' Olympic Champion ever (behind Sonja Henie and Barbara Ann Scott). It was in no small part due to her winning these first globally telecast Winter Olympics (which were also the first Winter Olympics to be broadcast live and in color) that she quickly turned pro and headlined *Ice Follies*.

She was recognized as perhaps the most charming ambassador skating has ever had, which might explain why Snoopy from the "Peanuts" comic strip once had a crush on her. Today she's still in public demand and remains at the forefront of skating, starring in traveling ice shows and serving as a sought-after television commentator for skating competitions.

In 1969, television audiences fell in love with a petite blonde pixie who had captured the U.S. Championship bronze medal the year before. For five years—from 1969 until 1973—Janet Lynn would be America's hope for the next worldwide ice queen. No other U.S. singles skater or team was nearly as dominant during this time. Three-time U.S. Champion Tim Wood won the silver medal at the 1968 Winter Olympics, and took the World titles in 1969 and 1970, but still was overshadowed by Lynn's radiance. Three-time U.S. Pairs Champions JoJo Starbuck and Kenneth Shelley won the World bronze medal in 1971 and 1972, achieving some fame during that time, but they experienced nothing like the adulation afforded Lynn.

Why was Lynn so popular? She won only two medals at the World Championships—a bronze in 1972 and a silver in 1973. She took the bronze medal at the 1972 Winter Olympics in Sapporo, Japan, yet was more popular than Beatrix Schuba, who won the gold.

Lynn was so poetic on the ice because she knew how to combine grace with athleticism. If Lynn had been competing under the rules that are in effect today, she would have won a number of World titles and the 1972 Olympics. She won many of the free programs, but she was not as good in figures. (Eight years later, Switzerland's Denise Biellmann encountered the same fate, placing fourth at the Lake Placid Winter Olympics after winning the nonfigures portions of the competition, because she was a dismal twelfth after the compulsory figures.)

At the 1972 Olympics, Beatrix "Trixi" Schuba, World silver medalist in 1969 and 1970 and World gold medalist in 1971 and

Her grace and gentleness on the ice made Peggy Fleming a skating idol for decades.

1972, was far ahead of Lynn and everyone else at the end of the compulsory figures. She was so far ahead, in fact, that she could afford to free skate as she usually did. And how she usually skated was generally considered to be rather lackluster and lifeless. It didn't matter that she placed ninth in the 1972 Worlds free skate (and it's generally considered that she wouldn't have medaled at all had it not been for her expertise at tracing figures). In 1972, the tracing of the figures (three times around each figure) accounted for a stunning 50 percent of a skater's total score. If someone racked up a big lead, it was hard for others to catch up.

This left Lynn in the lurch. Even though she was the best freestyle skater on the planet, adored by all, she could never overcome the tyranny of the figures. This helped add to the public's sympathy for her. And entering the free skate after being fourth in figures in Sapporo, she was so far above everyone else in grace, athleticism, and poise that she won the event even though she fell. And when she fell, she got up, smiling as if she had just landed the biggest jump ever, and continued. This endeared her even more to the public. Falling and still winning. Winning and still coming in third. The public loved Lynn and hated the system that allowed mediocre freestyle skating to win.

Janet Lynn did not retire after the Olympics. She stayed "eligible" for one more year, partially because compulsory school figures were being devalued to 30 percent of the overall score. A "short" freestyle skate program of required elements was added in 1973. At the 1973 Worlds, Lynn placed second behind Canada's Karen Magnussen, who had moved up from silver at Worlds the year before and bronze the year before that. Lynn had tripped up during the required jumps of the short program. The short program should have been her salvation, but instead, she placed a miserable twelfth leading into the long program. And then, with her typical come-from-behind, can-do spirit, she won the long program, the one that the worldwide television audience would actually see.

The poetic
Janet Lynn

Lynn would not get the crown many thought was due her, but others realized, gold medal or not, that she was ripe for public adoration. Chicago sports promoter Arthur M. Wirtz, who thirty-seven years earlier had signed up Sonja Henie, knew just how valuable Lynn was, no matter where she placed. He signed her to a $1.45 million deal with *Ice Follies*, making her the highest paid female athlete up to that time. Unfortunately, Lynn developed a severe case of asthma and had to retire from exhibitions before her contract expired.

Consummate Artists: Cranston and Curry

The always innovative Toller Cranston changed the face of skating.

Perhaps the most artistically influential skater of the day was Toller Cranston, Canadian Men's Champion for six years in a row, from 1971 to 1976. His only World medal was a bronze in 1974, and in 1976, he received the bronze medal at the Winter Olympics in Innsbruck. Like Janet Lynn, Cranston could have won the World Championships in 1974 and 1975 if not for his poor showing in figures, even though figures had been devalued.

Cranston's style was often more appreciated than understood. His choreography utilized movements, especially in spins, that were sculptural in character. He would transform his spinning body into unique contortions that had never been seen before. His captivating choreography and attention to musical detail made him far more influential than his medal count would suggest, sending skating off in an entirely new direction. He is, without a doubt, the most important skater never to win a World or Olympic gold medal.

Great Britain's John Curry won his first World medal, a bronze, in 1975. Then, in 1976, he won the gold medal at the Olympics and the World Championships. Because much of the television audience prior to the 1990s mostly paid attention to skating only during Olympic years, his 1976 Olympic gold was well timed. So was his decision to train under Carlo Fassi (Peggy Fleming's and Dorothy Hamill's coach) and Gustav Lussi (Dick Button's coach) when it appeared he wasn't moving up as he should in the World Championship rankings.

Curry had long felt that if he could win the Olympics, he would have the ability to take skating off in a new direction when he turned pro. His style was one of pure elegance, heavily influenced by the classical world of ballet. Every detail of his body position was important, down to his fingertips. He wanted to bring ballet to the ice and introduce fans to a new way of looking at figure skating, trusting in their ability to understand and appreciate subtlety and nuance. It would be a hard enough sell even if he did have an Olympic gold medal. Without it, his dream would die before it even got off the ground. But he pursued his ideal, turning down lucrative offers to skate in the more popular ice shows.

As a result of his victory in Innsbruck, Curry was able to pull together a troupe of skaters known as *The John Curry Theatre of Skating*. They brought ballet on ice to audiences in London in 1978 and 1979. Late in 1979, the ensemble came to the United States as *Ice Dancing*. Critics heaped rave reviews on the production, but it had to fold, as it continually lost money. Curry found that the American public might not be ready for what he had to offer.

The John Curry Skating Company was born in 1983, based on the concept of the earlier productions, but with better funding. The ensemble toured the world and performed to live orchestral music,

as Curry felt that the shows would not be as effective with taped music. (In that regard, he repeated what Jackson Haines had done about 120 years earlier.) From Japan to London to the United Arab Emirates and a series of opera houses and cultural centers in the United States, Curry showed audiences that skating could be a thing of pure beauty at a time when other ice shows were putting cartoon characters on the ice.

Curry commissioned some of the leading choreographers of the day to create new and daring works for the ice. Normally, one thinks of a figure skating choreographer as someone who works with a number of figure skaters, helping them develop their own unique and personal style on the ice. Curry went a step further in his desire to turn skating into an art form. He commissioned works for the ice from choreographers in the world of dance, people who had never before worked with figure skaters. These "outside" choreographers found it a challenge to work in the medium of skating. Their standard dance techniques did not allow for gliding across the surface of a stage. But in getting these creative forces to bring their talents to the ice, Curry forged new ideas that henceforward influenced all facets of skating.

Hamill and the Late 1970s

The last of Janet Lynn's five U.S. Championship gold medals was earned in 1973. In second place was Dorothy Hamill, who, like Fleming and Curry, was coached by the legendary Carlo Fassi. Hamill went on to win the next three U.S. titles and the 1976 Winter Olympics and World Championship.

Hamill had a different type of personality from Lynn's. Whereas Lynn was self-assured and confident, Hamill was always nervous before competitions, to the point that her coach couldn't help wondering if she would hold it all together until she got through her program. But television audiences saw her as being the innocent "girl next door," and they loved her for it.

John Curry brought the lyrical classicism of ballet to singles skating.

Olympic gold medalist Dorothy Hamill

In Munich (then in West Germany) in 1974, she was to skate her long program immediately after a West German favorite performed. Just as she was coming onto the ice, the audience started booing the scores of the previous skater. Hamill took the boos personally, broke down on the ice, and had to go to the side of the rink to be comforted by her coach. The audience, realizing what had happened, gave her a tremendous ovation upon her return, possibly giving her the strength to pull off her first World Championship medal, a silver.

She had two trademarks. One was the Hamill Camel, in which she would spin with her torso bent parallel to the ice and then drop into a sit spin. The other trademark was her compact, bowl-like Hamill Wedge hairstyle, which became a fad with schoolgirls throughout the United States.

After leaving amateur competition, Hamill skated for *Ice Capades*. In 1991, she bought the company in an attempt to save it from dissolving. During her tenure at the helm, the company became more balletlike, telling a continuous story instead of performing several unconnected routines. "Cinderella" and "Hansel and Gretel" captivated audiences, but they weren't the glitzy, gaudy showgirl spectacles that people had come to associate with the company. A few years later, she sold it.

Along the way, Hamill has become a television producer and still makes special appearances with a variety of skating shows.

Charles Tickner was the dominant force in American Men's skating in the late 1970s.

Toward the end of the 1970s, Charles Tickner became the dominant force in American Men's skating, winning the U.S. title in 1977, 1978, 1979, and 1980. Tickner placed on the medal stand at Worlds only twice, winning the gold in 1978 and the bronze in 1980, the same year he took bronze at the Lake Placid (New York) Winter Olympics behind Great Britain's Robin Cousins.

Despite Tickner's winning the 1978 World Championship in Ottawa, Canada, the big news in the Men's competition was a Canadian skater who didn't even make it to the podium. Vern Taylor executed the first successful triple axel—the three-and-a-half-revolution triple jump that's the most difficult of all—in competition at the Worlds. With all the triples now out of

the way, skaters could start dreaming about someday pulling off the "impossible" quad jump.

The same year of Taylor's accomplishment, Switzerland's Denise Biellmann became the first woman to pull off a triple lutz in competition.

Linda Fratianne won the U.S. Ladies' gold the same four years as Tickner took the U.S. Men's, and won the World gold medal twice, in 1977 and 1979, plus the silver in 1978 and the bronze in 1980. She took the silver medal behind Anett Pötzsch of the German Democratic Republic (GDR, or East Germany).

Despite winning Ladies' gold at the 1980 Winter Olympics, Pötzsch couldn't capitalize on the glamour of being the Olympic ice queen because of the restrictions of her country's communist political system. The leaders of the GDR (known almost exclusively as East Germany by North Americans and Western Europeans) believed that commercialism was an evil of American capitalism. Making money off one's talent was not in keeping with the spirit of socialism.

For the most part, star athletes from the communist countries weren't allowed to travel freely after their amateur days were over, for fear they would defect to the West. The authorities wanted to prevent defections such as that of the Soviet Pairs team of Ludmila and Oleg Protopopov (known in their amateur days as Belousova and Protopopov). They had won four World golds (1965–1968) and two Olympic golds (1964 and 1968) with their beautiful grace. After their 1980 defection to Switzerland, they became big hits on the ice show tour circuit and in professional contests. More unfortunate in the eyes of the communist authorities, they became vocal and eloquent spokespersons against the communist system. Therefore, star athletes from Soviet bloc nations who traveled to the West knew that their movements were being monitored. They also feared that a defection could have negative implications for family members back home.

Anett Pötzsch, despite having a personality Western audiences

Oleg and Ludmila Protopopov achieved World and Olympic fame as Belousova and Protopopov.

loved and an appreciation for American music—her 1980 Olympic closing ceremony exhibition performance was set to Louis Armstrong's music—would have few of the opportunities that were available to American Ladies' Olympic Champions such as Peggy Fleming and Dorothy Hamill.

Soviets Dominate Pairs and Ice Dancing

Ice Dancing wasn't recognized as an official event at the World Championships until 1952 and didn't become an Olympic event until 1976.

From 1952 through 1960, and from 1966 through 1969, every World Ice Dancing Championship was won by British teams.

Then, in 1970, Liudmila Pakhomova and Aleksandr Gorshkov, who have the most World Championship titles, with six, started a remarkable string of Soviet and, later, Russian victories. Soviet/Russian teams won every Ice Dancing World title through 1979 and twelve of the next eighteen titles up through 1997. Soviet/Russian teams also won five of the first six Ice Dancing titles given at the Winter Olympics, the one exception being Jayne Torvill and Christopher Dean's incredible year in 1984.

In Pairs skating, the Soviet/Russian skaters were also stunningly successful. Belousova and Protopopov's four World and two Olympic titles were followed by the dynasty of Irina Rodnina, who favored athleticism and more difficult side-by-side jumps. She won the first of her ten World Championships in 1969 with partner Alexsei Ulanov, winning three more Worlds in a row with him, as well as the 1972 Olympic crown. However, he fell in love with another Soviet skater, so she began to audition other male skaters with whom she could form a new partnership. With Alexandr Zaitsev, her future husband, she won the Worlds six years in a row, from 1973 through 1978, taking time off in 1979 to have a child. They also won the 1976 Olympics and, after she recovered from having her baby, came back and won the 1980 Olympics as well.

After Rodnina and Zaitsev retired, Soviet/Russian Pairs skaters won eleven of the next fourteen World Championships.

What is it about the Soviets that made them so dominant in Ice Dancing and Pairs? Some have argued that the system they lived under fostered a better competitive environment, that the Soviet skaters were given everything they needed for success—coaches, choreographers, ice time, a place to live, food—while the American skaters were forced to seek public and private sponsorships in order to stay in training. Also, numerous Ice Dancing and Pairs teams behind the former Iron Curtain were married. Many felt that their married status gave them quite an important advantage over most Western skating couples.

In Pairs and Ice Dancing, the man is responsible for showing off the woman. She is the main attraction, he the supporting cast. In

Pairs, he lifts and she rises above his shoulders. He throws and she sails through the air. Both Pairs and Ice Dancing couples have to convince the judges that they are two people united as one, a couple as opposed to two individuals. They have to demonstrate their caring for each other and show great emotion for each other on the ice. It's natural to suspect that married couples would have an easier time convincing judges of their bond. According to this line of thought, the Soviets must have had an advantage. This did nothing to explain, though, why so many unmarried Soviet skating couples were so successful at climbing to the top.

Maia Usova and Alexander Zhulin were among the many Soviet couples who got married partly for economic reasons.

In 1995, several years after the Soviet domination of Pairs and Ice Dancing commenced, Soviet/Russian Ice Dancer Alexander Zhulin (partner with Maia Usova) talked about this perception. They were third at the 1990 and 1991 Worlds, second in 1992, and first in 1993, as well as recipients of the bronze medal at the 1992 Winter Olympics and silver medal at the 1994 Olympics. Like so many other Soviets, they were married. And then they got divorced, as did so many ex-Soviet skating teams after the Soviet Union dissolved.

Zhulin states: "It's true that many, many Russian skating couples were married and now many, many Russian couples are divorced. The reason, actually, is very simple. I think fifty percent of the couples married because we Russians had nothing—no money, no anything. When they put their money together, they could buy a car, maybe afford a house, or get an apartment.

"Before we married, we got only one hundred rubles a month to skate. That's about twenty dollars of U.S. money. If we were married, we could get an apartment from our [skating] federation. As a married couple, we could get a letter from the federation that would be sent to the government. The letter would go to the government, who would then consider giving us a car so we could get to our training sessions easier and hopefully an apartment so we could have a normal life. Apartments are scarce, so they would rather give one out to a married couple than two to two singles.

"We took a train every day to practice that took one and a half hours each way. We couldn't get a place to stay any closer. And we ate like two dogs. I saw a movie over here in the U.S. about a prison, and all I could concentrate on was the prisoners were eating all this wonderful food.

"We couldn't understand how it was possible for people to live as they did in the United States and West Germany. Going to any city was like going to Disneyland."

So, as it turns out, things weren't all that rosy behind the Iron Curtain. What, then, explains the Soviet/Russian success in Pairs and Ice Dancing for so very long? We see it was difficult to live and train under their system. And yet, incredible Pairs and Ice Dancing couples kept capturing medal after medal.

Perhaps their skaters won so many medals because—and this may be a novel thought to some—they trained harder and ended up being better than everyone else.

Big Changes

Three Cheers for Artistry

I N A PERFECT WORLD, athleticism and artistry in figure skating would be mutually compatible. Over the years, however, skaters, judges, and the International Skating Union have been trying to come to grips with balancing the two ideals.

One year after placing fourth at the Winter Olympics despite winning the short and long programs at the event (because of a poor performance in figures), Switzerland's Denise Biellmann won the 1981 Worlds gold medal and then promptly turned pro. She never had a problem delivering both athleticism and artistry.

Her flexibility was legendary, and everyone waited through each of her routines for her crowning achievement, the "Biellmann Spin." With one leg extended above and behind her head, she looked like a revolving Christmas tree ornament. Such

Denise Biellmann demonstrates the spin that is her trademark.

grace was pure artistry, and such flexibility was the envy of any athlete. Her departure from the ranks of amateur Ladies' skaters left a vacuum. The door was open for less-rounded skaters to specialize as either artists or technicians.

It seems that whenever skaters and their coaches figure out how to pull off bigger and more challenging jumps, artistry has taken a temporary backseat. When one skater perfects a new jump for the first time, everyone else has to learn it so as not to be left behind. When Dick Button did the first triple jump, it wasn't long before every Men's skater was expected to do a triple. It wasn't long after Denise Biellmann became the first Ladies' competitor to execute a triple lutz in 1978 that all Ladies' hopefuls were polishing up their own triple lutzes. The same goes for Pairs lifts and throws and side-by-side jumps. Whoever does something for the first time is not going to be alone for long.

Near the end of the 1970s, more Ladies' entrants were experimenting with increased athleticism, often at the expense of artistry. One skater who refused to sell out her artistry was Lisa-Marie Allen, U.S. silver medalist during the last three years of Linda Fratianne's reign as U.S. Ladies' Champion (1978–1980),

Lisa-Marie Allen stressed beauty of movement over athleticism.

and bronze medalist behind Elaine Zayak in 1981. (She had stayed an amateur one year past the Olympics so she could go out as National Champion, then sprained her ankle and had to skate the long program with it wrapped.)

To many, Allen was the supreme musical stylist on the ice for her time. Like John Curry's, her every movement was smooth and understated. She did not call attention to herself through flashy and meaningless movements—instead she allowed her choreography to "breathe." She put in no movement unless it emphasized the mood of the moment in the music. Allen didn't jump just for the sake of jumping. At 5-9, she was able to exploit height without the biggest jumps.

She was inspired by the artistry of Peggy Fleming, whom she saw skate in *Ice Follies* as a birthday treat. The image of Fleming's grace never left her mind. During Allen's amateur career, increased demands of athleticism started to creep into Ladies' routines. Allen was disturbed by the trend of skaters' spending much of their programs doing little more than setting up big jumps instead of concentrating on creating beautiful lines with their stroking and lovely images with their entire bodies.

Increasingly, there seemed to be little demand for a skater who could melt one's socks off with style but who wouldn't jump unnecessarily if it would cheapen her program. Audiences were enamored of the jump-jump-jumping of tiny Elaine Zayak and seemed to be caring less for Fleming-like beauty and grace. As soon as she finished the 1981 season, with Zayak setting the course for the future of Ladies' skating in America, Allen packed her bags and joined *Ice Capades*.

At this writing, Allen is making quite a name for herself on the professional circuit and is in demand in pro competitions and ice shows, where style and grace are still rewarded. She is also active as co-founder and artistic director of City of Angels Ice Theatre, dedicated to developing the theatrical art form component of skating.

Elaine Zayak
ushered in an
athletic revolution
in Ladies' skating.

Three Cheers for Athleticism

While Allen was the perfect representative of skating as an art, Elaine Zayak was the anointed representative of the new ideal, the self-propelled jumping machine. U.S. gold medalist in 1981, bronze medalist in 1982 and 1984, and silver medalist in 1983 (the last three years behind Rosalynn Sumners), she burst onto the World Championships scene by taking the silver medal in 1981 and the bronze in 1984 and, most important, by her shocking win in 1982.

The press, always looking for a story even when one wasn't there, tried to make Zayak and Sumners out to be bitter rivals. Things got so silly in 1982 that the two skaters issued a joint "friendship statement" to try to put the inaccurate rumors of their alleged disdain for each other to rest.

Sumners was quite an adept technician who seemed at times to be unsure of herself. She was one of the first to admit using a sports psychologist to help her focus on her routine. In that regard, she was something of a pioneer. Sports psychologists are not at all uncommon today, as skaters strive to get every advantage they can over their competitors.

Despite winning the U.S. title in 1982, 1983, and 1984, and the World title in 1983, Sumners was haunted by persistent doubts of her ability to execute certain jumps flawlessly. At the 1984 Winter Olympics, she was on her way to winning the gold medal over Katarina Witt in the long program when she singled a double axel, doubled a triple toe loop combination, and then completely eliminated a triple toe loop and double axel. The

Rosalynn Sumners could jump flawlessly when not plagued with self-doubt.

result was that she lost the gold by the scantiest of margins—.1 from one judge.

But while Sumners had problems psychologically dealing with jumps she could normally do in her sleep, Zayak loved to jump and did so with effortlessness and abandon, as no rules were in place to stop her from jumping from one end of the rink to the other. The audiences loved it and the judges found they had no choice but to reward her for performing difficult jumps, even if she did them at the expense of artistry.

Feeling pushed by Zayak, other skaters started to pack more triples into their program, whether they fit or not. Falling during one's competition performance became more of a common occurrence. This was at no time any clearer than at the 1982 Worlds in Copenhagen, Denmark. Ladies' entrants were wiping up the ice in rehearsals, attempting jumps they could not yet control. All knew that Zayak's show was packed with triples.

She didn't appear to be much of a threat after taking tenth place in the short program, having a rather miserable time trying to keep things together. This dropped her to seventh overall, factoring in her placement in compulsory figures. In the long program, though, the unthinkable happened. One by one, each of the Ladies' entrants went out on the ice and, trying to keep up with the push toward athleticism, proceeded to fall, and fall, and fall during the "jump fest." Zayak, recovered from her short program, went onto the rink and gave the skating world a lesson in jumping, delivering seven perfect triples and becoming the only top skater to stay on her blades. She was the new World Champion.

The call became louder and louder from those concerned that artistry would disappear under an avalanche of jumps. Already, artistic creativity was suffering as skaters fell into the trap of "1-2-3-jump, 1-2-3-jump." In response, the International Skating Union passed a rule that sought to restore balance to the competition programs.

Under this rule, programs could not contain duplicate triples, although one triple could be done again if it was part of a combination jump. Skaters were also required to do a minimum number of spins and step sequences. The ISU action became informally known as the Zayak Rule.

Arguably, skaters develop technique before artistry, which is why young "jumping machine" skaters tend to be less artistic than older, more mature, and more developed skaters.

Some people with the ISU thought the Zayak Rule would be the last word needed to preserve artistry for all eternity. They did not realize that the ever-decreasing age of Ladies' competitors would send the average age of various nations' world teams spiraling downward.

Just What Is Ice Dancing?

While the big question in Ladies' singles skating during the early 1980s was "Is figure skating a sport or an art?" the big question in Ice Dancing during the same period appeared to be "What is Ice Dancing? Is it ballroom dancing on ice, or can it be something more?"

There are many restrictions in Ice Dancing. For starters, there are no big lifts over the man's head or dramatic throws, as with Pairs. There are no individual elements wherein one partner is apart from the other for several seconds, doing something individualistic, as is allowed in Pairs competition. The couples, for the most part, are always together, skating as a single entity instead of as two people with distinct roles. Footwork—how the feet interact with each other and move—is of far more importance than with Pairs.

Ice Dancing wasn't even an Olympic sport until 1976 and has been recognized at Worlds only since 1952, while there has been a Pairs event since 1908 at both the Olympics and Worlds. It was as if the authorities at the top levels of figure skating at first didn't want Ice Dancing in the world-level competitions at all and, once it was in, they didn't know how to handle it.

For quite some time, the changing of the guard in Ice Dancing had been moving at a glacial pace. Ice Dancing judging was accused of being much too predictable. It seemed that one could see who was going to win in future years by who was next in line. Case in point: At the 1984 Winter Olympics, Great Britain's Jayne Torvill and Christopher Dean won the gold (and then turned pro), followed by two teams from the Soviet Union, Natalia Bestemianova and Andrei Bukin (silver) and Marina Klimova and Sergei Ponomarenko (bronze). At the 1988 Winter Olympics, Bestemianova and Bukin won the gold (and then turned pro), and Klimova and Ponomarenko took the silver. Care to guess who won at the 1992 Winter Olympics?

At Worlds during that same period, things weren't much different. Bestemianova and Bukin waited in third one year and second for three years while Torvill and Dean won in 1981, 1982, 1983, and 1984. Then Bestemianova and Bukin moved up to first in 1985, 1986, 1987, and 1988, each year followed by Klimova and Ponomarenko in second. To no one's surprise, it was Klimova and Ponomarenko's turn on the top podium in 1989, 1990, and 1992, interrupted only by France's brother-and-sister team of Isabelle and Paul Duchesnay in 1991, as the Soviets temporarily took second.

The rankings of Ice Dancing couples were utterly predictable. And because there are no throws or high lifts in the sport, there was little mystery about whether or not a team would get through its program in one piece, unless the team members were to do something dramatic like skate into the wall and not come back to the ice. If a couple were to fall, they might as well pack up and go home. Otherwise, positions seldom changed from one phase of a competition to the next.

To many television viewers, one dance couple looked about the same as any other. The music seemed stuck in the ballrooms of Johann Strauss's nineteenth-century Vienna. There was little variety in styles from one couple to another, and watching the skaters go through the motions of traditional Ice Dancing was about as exciting as watching paint dry.

That all changed with the ascension of Jayne Torvill and Christopher Dean.

And Just Who Do Torvill and Dean Think They Are?

When Torvill and Dean won their first of four straight World titles in 1981, it's doubtful that many had any idea of the extent to which they would shake things up. They hadn't shattered any Ice Dancing stereotypes earlier. It had been too important for them to get established first. Unknown to the world at large, Dean had quite a vivid imagination and was remarkably creative—a surprise to some, because most of the ideas in their earlier days are said to have come from Torvill. In 1982, the team created a free dance program to *Mack and Mabel,* a musical. If they hadn't had the previous year's gold to back them up, the judges might not have accepted the program as well as they did. Instead of straight-ahead ballroom dancing on ice, Torvill and Dean created a unified theme, and each became one of the two lead characters.

Today, that doesn't sound like such a big deal. In 1982, it was on the verge of heresy. But the judges couldn't argue with Torvill and Dean's impeccable technique and stunning choreography. The team, more than any other, redefined choreography as something more than just movement on the ice to music. Torvill and Dean *became* the music. Instead of simply interpreting the music, they

Jayne Torvill and Christopher Dean are the greatest Ice Dancers of all time.

brought new meaning to it by pouring their personalities into it. They didn't keep their distance from the music—they chopped it, diced it, pureed it, and shaped it into a presence of their own creation. They put the stamp of their unique personalities upon the music. This was radical for Ice Dancers of the time.

In 1983, Torvill and Dean presented the musical *Barnum*, bringing a spontaneous circus flair to the ice. The program didn't seem cut and dried; it seemed to evolve anew every time it was skated. And indeed, Torvill and Dean became well known for changing programs up to the last possible moment. Near the end of the program, Dean spun Torvill around the ice like a toy top. The audience at Worlds went bonkers. There was nothing in the rule book to stop them, and indeed they relished staying ahead of the restrictive Ice Dancing rules—not breaking them, but stretching them to the limits.

They were awarded perfect 6.0s in Presentation from all nine judges. They were unquestionably the favorites heading into the 1984 Winter Olympics, but no one at the time could have guessed just what a dramatic impact they would have on the sport one year later.

The year 1983 also produced one of the strangest things ever to happen in Ice Dancing; however, because it happened behind the scenes, few people were aware of it at the time. At Worlds, the designated Original Set Pattern Dance was to be skated to a rock and roll tempo. (For this part of the competition, all dance teams must create a repetitive dance, performed to the same style of music. The style is announced months in advance, giving each team the chance to choose its own musical selection within the framework of the style.)

Canada's Tracy Wilson and Robert McCall decided to perform their Original Set Pattern Dance to the music of Paul Anka. Earlier in the season, international judges told them that their musical selection wasn't rock and roll. A deposition from famed rock and roll singer and songwriter Anka convinced the judges otherwise, and

Wilson and McCall were able to keep the music, without penalty.

Another 1983 judging call was just plain weird. Five-time U.S. Champions (1981–1985) Judy Blumberg and Michael Seibert were told at Worlds by an Italian judge that their Fred Astaire/Ginger Rogers music was "not dance music." *Not dance music?* Tell that to the millions of people in dance halls who have danced the night away to the same music. This judge dumped them because of her opinion, but they still managed to finish with the bronze, as they would do again in 1984 and 1985.

Judy Blumberg and Michael Seibert were one of America's strongest Ice Dancing teams.

For the 1984 Winter Olympics in Sarajevo, Yugoslavia, Blumberg and Seibert put together a dramatic portrait on ice based on the dynamic Mussorgsky tone poem *Scheherazade*. It was not a typical dance program, but it was within the boundaries that were being expanded by Torvill and Dean. The dance team was on its way to winning a silver medal at the Olympics when the same judge who dumped them in 1983 did so again, stating that she didn't like the music, which had already been approved by an international panel. This action knocked Blumberg and Seibert all the way to fourth place. At Worlds a month later, the team did not skate nearly as well as at the Olympics, even by their own admission. Yet they took the bronze. In some ways, this made the Olympic situation hurt even more, as it proved to them that they had been worthy of winning an Olympic medal.

Bolero *and Beyond*

But 1984 will forever be remembered for Torvill and Dean's landmark *Bolero* free dance program, set to the music of Maurice Ravel's famous orchestral work. Perhaps the most heralded program ever presented on the ice, it took the theme concept a step further, since it used a single piece of music instead of snippets from multiple selections. A single repetitive musical statement began softly and continually built to the dynamic conclusion. There were no tempo changes—which was unheard of—and the musical and choreographic flow was continuous.

With *Bolero,* Torvill and Dean didn't just give Ice Dancing a nudge—they pushed it over the cliff.

For several seconds at the beginning, they didn't even skate. Dean, kneeling on the ice, twisted Torvill into several contortions as if he were playing with a stick of licorice. Then, when they stood up to skate, time itself seemed to disappear. Their movements were fluid and seamless. Everything blended from one moment to the next. It was hypnotic to watch, and one was afraid to breathe, lest one ruin the aura of the moment. It was, in short, magic.

At the end, Dean twisted Torvill back and forth in the air, off to his front and side, being careful not to lift her too high, which would violate the rules. It was the closest thing to a Pairs "trick" that Ice Dancing had ever seen, and yet it was perfectly legal. As in 1983, they received nine perfect 6.0s in Presentation, and they added three perfect 6.0s in their technical marks.

Torvill and Dean went on to have a successful professional career and they toured the world with several shows of their own design, continuing to expand the art form and taking Ice Dancing more toward a concept of Ice Theater. Ten years after they changed the face of Ice Dancing, they reinstated as amateurs in order to compete in the 1994 Winter Olympics.

Natalia Bestemianova and Andrei Bukin exploited their flair for the dramatic.

By 1985, the ISU had started to restrain innovation in Ice Dancing, and the sport became more restrictive and headed back to its ballroom roots. Although theatrical presentations were popular with audiences, the ISU officials were concerned that Ice Dancing was selling out and losing its heritage.

Bestemianova and Bukin (popularly known as B&B) won all the World Championships from 1985 through 1988, as well

The sensual and expressive Marina Klimova and her husband, Sergei Ponomarenko

as the 1988 Winter Olympics. They had a wonderfully dramatic flair. Some criticized them for being too flamboyant, with movements that were extremely exaggerated and theatrical. Klimova and Ponomarenko took over the helm in 1989, 1990, and 1992, also winning the 1992 Winter Olympics. The married couple (especially Klimova) brought a searing passion into the rink, just about melting the ice with their obvious love for each other. Though far more ballroom-oriented than Torvill and Dean, they managed to sell their style to the public through their passion.

During the post–Torvill and Dean years, the British team's influence was kept alive by the Ice Dancing brother-and-sister team of Isabelle and Paul Duchesnay, who left Canada to skate for France. Dean choreographed their programs, and the Duchesnays became famous for many unusual body positions. (Dean ended up marrying Isabelle, but the marriage didn't work out. Later, he married 1990 Ladies' Champion, Jill Trenary.)

What Dean came up with in 1988 shocked just about everyone. The *Savage Rites* jungle program the Duchesnays took to the 1988 Winter Olympics found them attired in jungle garb, shocking a number of judges, who were used to pretty dresses and nondescript male attire.

The audience at the European Championships was thrilled to the point of throwing seat cushions in the air, but some judges were aghast at this "impure" intrusion upon their sacred ground. They placed the Duchesnays eighth at the Winter Olympics, proving that they didn't know how to judge the routine by giving them scores that varied by .8 in Presentation. In amateur figure skating events, where judges have only six points to work with, that's a chasm as wide as the Grand Canyon.

Paul remembers why the team made such a dramatic departure from the norm. "Change in Ice Dancing is a slow process. Normally you wait for the ones in front of you to retire and then you will move up ahead. However, our amateur career didn't last that long.

To go from twelfth [in 1986] to first [in 1991 with *Missing II*, a show inspired by political oppression in South America], we had to create a little bit of a ruckus."

Many expected the team to win the 1992 Winter Olympics, but an operation on Isabelle's foot just a few months before and problems with the French skating federation made things difficult for them. They ended up settling for second behind Klimova and Ponomarenko with a somewhat more traditional (for them) *West Side Story* program that was not their first choice.

Paul talks further of the mind-set among the day's rule makers. "We came up with our first musical choices, and the federation said, 'No, that won't do. It's too much.' The International Skating Union said, 'You have to change music because if you use this you will not win.'

"We asked the referee who was going to judge the music in Albertville [scene of the Olympics], and he said, 'If you choose this music, you will not be in contention. I will personally [Paul then made a slashing movement with his finger across his throat].' Things were difficult because we were forced to use conventional music."

After the 1992 Winter Olympics, Isabelle commented on the Ice Dancing restrictions by stating that the ISU should throw away the rule book. She added, "I think they should throw it away because it's hindering Ice Dancing. There are too many rules regarding music, costuming, and choreography. You don't have the freedom to pick what you want. The innovation is erased before we even start, and we don't have as much variety to pick from as we could. The girl has to wear a skirt; the music can only be ballroom-type with a rhythm."

It's as if the Torvill and Dean revolution never happened.

Good-bye to Figures

The death of compulsory figures was a long and painful one—long for the number of years it took, painful for skaters such as Janet

Judges often didn't know how to respond to the daring costumes and innovative choreography of Isabelle and Paul Duchesnay.

Lynn and Denise Biellmann, who swept the free skate portions of major competitions yet were prevented from winning some titles by their level of expertise in tracing mundane figures.

Up until 1968, compulsory figures were worth 60 percent of a single skater's total score. In 1968, they were reduced to 50 percent. The reduction was the first gasp in the death of figures, but they still accounted for half the score. This explained why someone like Beatrix Schuba could win three major titles despite not even placing in the top six in any of the free skate segments of the competitions.

Figures also gave judges a chance to hold back skaters they didn't like, regardless of how well they performed in that first segment of the competition. It's been said that sometimes certain judges "propped up" their favorite skaters (or skaters from their home country) with high marks in the compulsories and "dumped on" their less favorite skaters (or skaters from other countries) with low marks.

Having to know dozens of variations on a figure eight—some of which had to be steadily traced on one foot, and then retraced twice perfectly over the first tracing—was a bore for singles skaters who really just wanted to go out and show the world how good they were and how much fun they were having.

There were many ways skaters could mess up a required figure: They could push off too lightly, causing them not to make it all the way around the tracing. This was considered "death" to a skater's chance of getting a good score. And the etching itself wasn't all that was scored by the judges. Also important was posture. Control and patience were two of the key elements required to get it just right.

Even at the World Championships, few fans would show up to watch the figures portion of the competition, unless they just wanted to get a glimpse of the top skaters. It was like watching a yacht race: One knew the skater was out there, but one couldn't really tell exactly what was happening.

After a skater traced each figure, the judges would closely observe the etching, getting on their knees if necessary, looking for every little bobble and mistake. Still, voices cried out for figures to be saved. They said that the countless hours spent tracing figures helped skaters learn control and techniques that would help them in free skating.

In 1973, the first short program was introduced. This program required singles skaters to execute specific jumps and use certain techniques, to music of their own choosing. With that, figures were reduced to 30 percent of the total score. In the 1980s, opponents of figures started to raise their voices, proclaiming that it was time to eliminate figures altogether. For 1989 and 1990, the ISU reduced figures to just 20 percent of the total score. Skaters still had to do them, but if they weren't all that good in the discipline, their chances wouldn't be killed entirely.

The last compulsory figures were executed at the 1990 Worlds in Halifax, Nova Scotia. With the elimination of the figures, the short program took on increased importance for singles skaters, counting for one-third of the overall score. If they miss any of the required elements, their chances for overall success can be doomed. With compulsory figures but a distant memory, the discipline seems to have gone the way of the dinosaur.

Big Personalities

Olympic Heartbreaks

FEW MOMENTS IN THE HISTORY OF U.S. FIGURE SKATING were as sad as the 1980 Winter Olympics nonperformance of Tai Babilonia and Randy Gardner, U.S. Pairs Champions from 1976 through 1980. Babilonia and Gardner were considered the country's best hope at Olympic gold in Pairs.

At both the 1976 Winter Olympics and Worlds, the year of their first U.S. Championship, the team placed a respectable fifth. They moved up to the bronze medal position in the next two years and won Worlds in 1979, the year ten-time World Champion Irina Rodnina took off to have a baby with her second partner and husband, Alexandr Zaitsev. Babilonia and Gardner's 1979 victory set them up, in the eyes of many, as the team with the most momentum going into the 1980 Olympics, especially because Rodnina and Zaitsev would be coming off a season of noncompetition.

There was something fresh-faced about Babilonia and Gardner, something very all-American. Most of the country's best wishes rested on the shoulders of the one couple who stood the best chance of breaking the Soviet domination of Pairs. Until Babilonia and Gardner's 1979 victory, Soviet Pairs had won every Worlds since 1965 and every Winter Olympics since 1964.

The Pairs 1980 Winter Olympics long program was about to begin. Because the two weeks of festivities were being held in Lake Placid, New York, there was more interest than usual from the American television audience. With cameras focused on the final warm-up session, the unthinkable happened in front of the eyes of the world. Gardner kept falling on the ice, grimacing in pain. Word of a prior muscle pull circulated, and the public watched in shock

Tai Babilonia and Randy Gardner will forever be remembered for their heartbreaking last-minute withdrawal from the Olympics.

as Gardner made it back to his coach and a confused Babilonia.

There was no way he could go through the program and risk serious injury to himself and his partner. At the eleventh hour, the pair had to withdraw from competition. Gardner left the ice in shock. Babilonia left in tears. Throughout the country, people watching on television also had tears in their eyes. The cruelest fate seemed to be to allow such a gifted couple, who had worked their entire lives for this moment, to get so close, yet stay so far away.

For years, skating commentators would refer to the pair as the Heartbreak Kids. They were always warmly received by fans in exhibitions and at pro competitions. But in the back of perhaps every fan's mind was one simple thought: What if?

Canadian skating fans had their own version of the Heartbreak Kids at the 1984 Olympics. Unlike Babilonia and Gardner in Lake Placid, Barbara Underhill and Paul Martini did get a chance to perform in Sarajevo, but what was to be their moment in the sun turned into disaster. Despite having just barely placed in medal position at the previous Worlds, they were perceived by many as having the best shot at winning the 1984 Winter Olympics.

Not long before the Olympics, Underhill changed her boots. This turned out to haunt the team, and they fell—literally—to seventh in Sarajevo. First, Underhill fell during a sit spin in the short program and took Martini down with her. At that moment, their Olympic dream was over. But sadly, things got worse. During the long program, Underhill fell again, and both partners took turns singling side-by-side double salchows.

Underhill went back to her old boots right after the Olympics, and the team went on to win Worlds a few weeks later with a stunning performance in Ottawa, Canada. The audience was cheering so loudly during the last minute that the music was almost drowned out.

Interestingly, the American team of Caitlin and Peter Carruthers's second place at the 1984 Winter Olympics was seen as a victory for them. Not given much of a chance even to medal, they sat in good

New boots proved to be the undoing of Olympic hopes for Barbara Underhill and Paul Martini.

Sister and brother Caitlin and Peter Carruthers became national heroes for their dynamic 1984 Olympic performance.

position after the short program and put on the performance of their lives in the long program. Many felt that they should have beaten Soviets Elena Valova and Oleg Vasiliev, so dynamic was their performance. Carruthers and Carruthers returned home to a heroes' welcome and were the focus of many subsequent ice show performances—not because they placed second in the Olympics, but because they did better than expected.

Ekaterina Gordeeva and Sergei Grinkov captured two Olympic gold medals.

Gordeeva and Grinkov

Soviet skaters Ekaterina Gordeeva and Sergei Grinkov were paired together when he was fifteen and she an incredibly young ten years old. Critics lambasted the pairing, saying that Grinkov was so much taller than Gordeeva that he could throw her around the ice like a rag doll. The criticism of the pair's height and age difference intensified when they won the World Championship in 1986 with many dramatic lifts and throws, but somewhat less successful artistry. But by 1987 and their second World Championship, their classical style started to shine through, leaving critics with little verbal ammunition. They went on to win the 1989 and 1990 Worlds as well and the 1988 Winter Olympics over defending Champions Valova and Vasiliev.

Still, success didn't spare them occasionally weird speculation on their age difference. In 1988, someone in the press asked Gordeeva if she would consider dumping Grinkov for a younger partner. Rather than break up over their physical differences, they fell in love and got married. But, unlike so many other Soviet skating couples, they stayed married, their love growing deeper every year. Their love was the genuine article, and even previous critics, now enamored of their beauty and grace on the ice, would have to admit that their relationship was a model for skating and nonskating couples alike.

After turning pro, the couple joined the *Stars on Ice* tour, continuing to polish and perfect their style even more. They moved to America, like so many other former Soviets, and became the proud parents of a baby girl, Daria, who was "adopted" by all the members of the tour.

When the ISU announced that the 1994 Winter Olympics would be open to professionals, Gordeeva and Grinkov reinstated and took another swing at amateur competition, their classical purity providing a contrast to the heartfelt drama and emotional soul-baring of defending Olympic Pairs Champions Natalia Mishkutenok and Artur Dmitriev. Both pairs were skating not for the now defunct Soviet Union but for their native Russia. Television skating commentator Dick Button mentioned that of all the professional skaters who were reinstating for the Olympics (among them Katarina Witt, Brian Boitano, Viktor Petrenko, Torvill and Dean, and Mishkutenok and Dmitriev), the reinstatement of G&G was the most viable.

Gordeeva and Grinkov won their second Olympic Championship and made big plans for the future. But in November 1995, tragedy struck when Grinkov collapsed and died during practice in Lake Placid for the upcoming *Stars on Ice* tour. Always appearing to be the picture of health, he had undetected severe congenital heart disease. A massive heart attack, with no warning, claimed the life of one of the most gentle people the world of skating has seen.

The skating world was stunned by the tragedy, but it was especially hard on the close-knit company of *Stars on Ice*. However, in true "the show must go on" fashion, the 1995–1996 tour opened less than two weeks later, minus the pair that best exemplified perfection.

After months of mourning, friends of Ekaterina (Katia), including the *Stars on Ice* cast, performed a televised memorial tribute to Sergei. At the beginning of the program, a lone spotlight grazed across the ice, following the invisible pair that was now but a memory. Sergei's skater friends took turns presenting their skating tributes, many of which were not at all sad, in keeping with the spirit of celebrating his life. Twice during the presentation, Katia took to the ice as a new singles skater, sharing her pain and her hope with the teary audience. It was one of the most courageous acts ever witnessed on ice. She knew Sergei would not want her to give up her love and passion for skating.

Hamilton: The "Little Giant"

It's impossible to find anyone who doesn't love Scott Hamilton. Perhaps the most popular skating personality today, he has long been considered the number one spokesperson for figure skating. Respected universally by his fellow skaters and the public, he is one voice that is always trusted as a TV skating commentator.

His exhibition programs—and, later, his professional programs—have long been noted for bringing humor into the rink. Few skaters have had the courage to recognize humor as a legitimate vehicle for serious skating. As film actors and actresses have long said, comedy is much more difficult to perform than "serious" acting, and this perhaps explains why Hamilton's unique sense of what will make people laugh is so special.

Hamilton took up skating partly as a way of overcoming the effects of a childhood illness, Shwachman's disease. The malady causes a failure to metabolize food, sometimes leading to starvation, and often results in lack of growth.

Stars on Ice founder Scott Hamilton has retained a sense of humor in life and on the ice.

Recognized as a fighter with a lot of heart, he was selected by his 1980 Olympic teammates to carry the American flag in the 1980 Winter Olympics Opening Ceremony in Lake Placid, when he was still a relatively unknown skater.

One year later, Hamilton would win the first of his four straight World Championships. In 1982, he became the first American skater since Tim Wood (1969 and 1970) to win back-to-back Worlds. He went on to win the 1983 and 1984 Worlds, as well as the 1984

Winter Olympics, over strong challenges by Canadian Brian Orser.

Hamilton did not win the compulsory figures portion of the 1981, 1982, and 1983 Worlds. Therefore, it came as a surprise to many when he not only placed first in figures at the 1984 Winter Olympics in Sarajevo but also did so with a massive lead. Orser placed seventh in figures, making his gold medal hunt extremely difficult.

Orser won both the short and long programs, and Hamilton presented a substantially less than stellar long program performance, singling a triple flip and doubling a triple salchow. Unknown to many at the time, this was largely the result of an annoying inner ear infection. (The inner ear controls one's sense of balance, something that is crucial to everyone but especially to skaters.)

The media being what they are, Hamilton was bombarded with questions as to whether he was embarrassed to win the gold medal with a sub-par performance. Realizing he was the first American man to win Olympic gold since David Jenkins in 1960, he responded, "I came here for the gold and I did it. It may not have been pretty, but I did it."

Enjoying a solid professional career, he has continued to skate dynamic programs full of zing and zest. Looking for another challenge, he went on to found *Stars on Ice*, a traveling ice show with a cast of famous skaters who often unite as an ensemble to tell a story with costumes, props, and creative lighting.

Then, in early 1997, he was diagnosed with cancer. The news hit during the 1997 Worlds, with the skating world still reeling from the sudden death earlier in the week of famed coach Carlo Fassi. Hamilton fought it hard, went through extensive therapy, and made his way back onto the ice. Later in the year, a televised tribute was held in his honor, featuring performances by many of his closest skating friends. Scott took to the ice at the end and amazed everyone by pulling off two of his famous back flips, demonstrating his courage and heart.

At the end of his performance, he grabbed the microphone and breathlessly proclaimed, "I win. I win." The battle he had won was far more significant than all four World golds and his Olympic gold medal combined.

Boitano: *The Artist Revealed*

When Brian Boitano first hit the world stage in 1983, it's doubtful that many people realized his impending greatness. Scott Hamilton said, about that time, that Boitano was the greatest jumper he had ever seen, so there was reason to keep an eye on him.

Twelve years prior to his first trip to Worlds, Boitano started group lessons with a local San Francisco–area coach, Linda Leaver, who was practically unknown outside of her rink. She recognized his potential so strongly that when her husband had a chance to be transferred to a better job, she persuaded him to turn it down so she could mold Boitano into the champion she was convinced he could become. Her husband agreed to give her a certain amount of time to see if her intuition was correct.

More than a quarter century later, Leaver remains the only coach Boitano has ever had. He stuck with her as he was ascending through the ranks, despite repeated suggestions from others that he should go work with a coach with more "experience." Boitano showed the same faith in Leaver that Leaver had showed in him and that Leaver's husband showed in her.

Along the way, Boitano would win the U.S. Championship from 1985 through 1988, the World Championship in 1986 and 1988, and the 1988 Winter Olympics, plus almost too many professional championships to count.

However, there seemed to be a problem. Boitano was, as Hamilton suggested, the best jumper in the world. His technique was impeccable. He usually did well in figures, and he was fearless in his desire to try jumps most other skaters would shy away from. But observers commented that he wasn't nearly as artistic as he should be.

It was the compulsory figures, which he loved, that would undo him during his first real shot at going to Worlds. In 1982, with Hamilton still riding high, Boitano missed a chance to make the World Team at the U.S. Nationals, a moment he says was his lowest point in skating. Because of a sixth-place finish in figures, he finished fourth place overall after nailing every triple in the book, including the triple axel. His short program was clean; he was the only one to execute a triple flip–triple toe loop combination at a time when double-triples just weren't being done. Also, his long program was a study in how to toss off triples as if they were child's play. But one mistake on one figure doomed his chances to move on, and he asked in frustration, "What do I need to do to make these people want to send me?"

What the skating world didn't know was how devastating that experience was to him at the time. He admits to having had thoughts of hanging up his skates.

In 1983 and 1984, he made the U.S. World Team, finishing seventh in 1983 and sixth in 1984 at Worlds, with a strong fifth-place finish at the 1984 Winter Olympics. He was the U.S. Men's Champion four years in a row, from 1985 through 1988. He moved up to third at Worlds in 1985, and stunned everyone at the 1986 Worlds by laying down a long program that was on the verge of perfection. His victory inspired him to try to be the first to successfully land a quad jump in world competition.

The 1987 Worlds received a lot of publicity in the United States, as they were held in Cincinnati, Ohio. The publicity largely centered on Boitano's attempt to nail the infamous quad toe loop—which was like the fabled Western jackelope, rumored to exist but never actually seen live.

Brian Orser had finished second at Worlds for three years in a row, also finishing second to Hamilton at the 1984 Winter Olympics. Cruelly nicknamed Mr. Second Place by somewhat insensitive skating commentators, he had much to prove in Boitano's

Brian Boitano's backward-leaning spread eagle is one of the most dramatic moves in figure skating.

home country. Orser lit the arena on fire in his short program, not just nailing jumps but also demonstrating his artistic superiority over Boitano—something not lost on coach Leaver.

Boitano had announced he was going to go for the quad in the long program, no matter what. A headline in one of the Cincinnati newspapers screamed out, QUAD LOOMS TONIGHT. Indeed, he had nailed the jump in the open practice session, and all knew he was capable of pulling it off. (To the untrained eye, the quad toe loop appears something like the three-and-a-half-revolution triple axel, but more of a blur. Many skating fans don't really care which edges set up the jumps and which ones land them. But they can recognize a big, big jump when they see it.)

In the long program, Boitano went for the quad as thousands of fans held their breath, and he fell out of it. Mr. Second Place had his first—and only—World Championship, getting the opportunity to retire the undesired nickname. Boitano had to settle for the silver medal. Later Boitano said, "If I had played it conservatively, I think I could have won that competition. But then I wouldn't have made any changes in my mind, in my brain, and then come back stronger the next year."

The changes he made were largely in his artistic approach. After the 1987 Worlds loss, when some analysts commented that he seemed mostly to be just going through the motions, with little care for how the motions were connected together, Leaver called in Canadian Sandra Bezic. Bezic was gaining a reputation as a choreographer sensitive to unleashing artistic senses within skaters, but her work with Boitano would establish her as a miracle worker. She released the artist within him, and less than a year later, Boitano was *the* artistic skater of the 1988 Winter Olympics.

The Olympics were being held in Orser's home country, which partially accounted for his decision to stay eligible after his loss to Hamilton at the big show in 1984. Both he and Boitano ended up doing military-themed presentations for the 1988 long program,

Brian Orser was a silver medalist at two consecutive Olympics.

allowing an even closer comparison of styles between the two—and encouraging the media to declare the Olympic matchup the Battle of the Brians.

When Boitano hit the U.S. Nationals, fans gasped. He wasn't just artistic, he was remarkably artistic, full of soulful energy and emotional delivery. Leaver's decision to "share" him with Bezic turned out to be just what he needed.

For his short program, Bezic choreographed a routine to the waltz music of *Les Patineurs* (*The Skaters*). After a difficult jump, Boitano was to reach down and wipe the ice shavings off his blade, and then casually toss the shavings over his shoulder as if saying, "No big deal." One could not help but make the comparison to tossing salt over one's shoulder for good luck.

Boitano performed no quad that year, but he did a new jump, the Tano triple lutz. He extended his arm above his head during the jump, as opposed to the standard practice of pulling one's arms into the body to help with the rotation. The extended arm seriously throws one's balance off center, making the jump difficult to control. But he did it spectacularly, as if to show that standard laws of physics did not apply to him. It has become a trademark of his.

By the time Boitano hit his lengthy spread eagle in the Olympic long program, with legs wide open and a backward-leaning position that seemed impossible to maintain for a second—not to mention for a complete circle around the rink—there was no doubt that he had transformed himself into a total artist. He won the Olympics with what was instantly described as a "performance of a lifetime," edging a near-solid performance by Orser (who had turned a triple Axel into a double). Orser must have felt as if he had been hit by a ton of bricks.

Oh, about the figure that doomed Boitano at the 1982 U.S. Nationals? It was also required at the 1988 Winter Olympics. He nailed it, perfectly, in one continuous line.

Boitano went on to win the 1988 Worlds over Orser and has since enjoyed one of the most remarkable professional careers ever. He's put together a number of touring events and has been involved in several televised skating shows, realizing that "more people in one night see a TV show than are going to see the entire tour live."

And he still is coached by Leaver whenever possible.

But, despite his victories, he refused to take his awards and go quietly into the night. Boitano became the leading spokesperson for the idea of allowing professional skaters to compete in the Olympics. When the ISU formally agreed to open up the 1994 Winter Olympics to professionals, the ruling became known informally as the Boitano Rule. He, naturally, was the first professional skater to decide to reactivate his eligibility. (We'll take a closer look at the 1994 Olympics in the next chapter.)

Today, people still talk about his remarkable 1988 Olympic performance as if it had taken place yesterday. Boitano reflects on the moment: "The interesting thing is, that was just a practice performance for me, a practice performance that I laid out in front of everybody. That's what was so fulfilling."

America's New Sweetheart Is Not from America

A case can be made that from 1984 through 1988, Katarina Witt was the most popular Ladies' skater among American fans. She had an appeal that was universal, she wasn't afraid to flaunt her femininity, and she was a shameless flirt on the ice. It's said that she received so many letters from male admirers that she had no place to store them except in her bathtub.

And, despite being so popular among Americans, she wasn't even an American skater. In fact, she was a citizen of the German Democratic Republic, more commonly known as East Germany. In many ways, her communist government placed far more restrictions on athletes than the Soviet Union did. But Witt enjoyed freedoms other citizens didn't enjoy, because the authorities realized her public relations value and allowed her unprecedented travel freedom.

She was second to Elaine Zayak at the 1982 Worlds, and at the 1983 Worlds, Witt placed second in the short program and won the long, but she slipped to fourth place overall because she finished eighth in figures. Witt went on to win the 1984 Winter Olympics in Sarajevo over Rosalynn Sumners and the 1984 Worlds over Elaine Zayak, establishing herself as a powerhouse and becoming one of the few figure skating "stories" to emerge from behind the drama of Torvill and Dean's *Bolero* Ice Dancing revolution. But while other top skaters were able to cash in on their Olympic successes, she was unable to do so. Her country's political system would not allow her to accept an offer to be a cover girl for an American cosmetics company.

She went on to win the 1985 Worlds and then slipped to second behind the athleticism of America's Debi Thomas in 1986. But she bounced back in 1987 and once again won the Winter Olympics, in Calgary in 1988, and that year's Worlds as well.

She knew how to work an audience unlike any other skater. At the 1987 Worlds in Cincinnati, she stuck around the auditorium where the compulsory figures competition was being held, going up into the stands to sign autographs. This action earned her a scolding, via the local newspapers, from the camp of Debi Thomas and her coach, Alex McGowan. They said she was trying to win American fans by being so accessible, to which many of those American fans probably responded with "And your point is . . . ?"

She didn't quiet these detractors by her next move, which some feel she planned. Every skater is allowed a block of time to be on the ice during a practice session hours before a free skate event. The music of each skater is played over the arena sound system. Although each skater is given a chance for a full run-through, few actually take the opportunity to do so. They might just skate around a bit to get a feel for the rink and try a few jumps, preferring to save their energy for the actual contest.

At the end of the practice session for the final group of Ladies' skaters, no one was left on the ice but Witt. There was still one more

Katarina Witt became one of the most popular skaters among American audiences.

skater's music selection to be played. The practice session audience started to call out for Witt to do something, and she responded by making up a routine on the spot to the other skater's music. Her movements seemed to fit perfectly. The audience ate it up, and Witt won many new fans.

The Thomas camp, which through the media was trying to get American fans to support Thomas, was not doing cartwheels.

Both skaters performed solid technical programs, but Witt had the edge in artistic marks. Thomas finished a strong second and helped set up a year-long anticipation of the 1988 Winter Olympics.

Ironically, there was a possibility that Witt might not have been allowed to perform at the 1987 Worlds. Each medalist from the four disciplines—Men's, Ladies', Pairs, and Ice Dancing—the year before was given a full-page color photo spread in the program book. Her photo caption identified her as being from East Germany. Officials of the German Democratic Republic demanded that the program book be altered or they would pull her from the competition. Thousands of stickers were printed up, and workers spent several hours frantically sticking them over the offending caption in every souvenir program book.

In 1988, both Witt and Thomas skated to music from the opera *Carmen* at the Calgary Winter Olympics. Witt proclaimed that while Thomas *skated* to music from *Carmen*, she (Witt) "*became* Carmen," the lead character from the opera.

She created controversy with a short program outfit that some felt was far too revealing of her thighs. She added feathers in "strategic" locations after the European Championships but still gave reason for people to talk about her. (And while they talked about her, good or bad, they weren't talking about anyone else. She was, after all, a master at media manipulation.) Thomas added fuel to the media fire by stating, a day before the Olympic long program, "Her costumes belong in an X-rated movie." A twenty-minute press conference with gaga media in Calgary focused on all the distractions, rather than on her skating. Witt was probably pleased with the attention.

She won her second Olympic gold medal despite a lengthy section in the middle of her program where she flirted more than she skated. But she didn't turn out to be the main talk of the Ladies' competition.

Canadian Elizabeth Manley, who had never stood on a Worlds medals podium, caught fire and electrified the largely Canadian audience in the short program, where she was a surprise third, and in the long program, which she won with an especially impressive performance. She took the Olympic silver medal, a fact that seemed hard for her to believe, as she bit the medal on the podium just to be sure it was real.

American hopeful Caryn Kadavy, bronze medalist from the 1987 Worlds, had to withdraw from the Olympics because of the flu, after valiantly competing in the short program. Fellow teammate Jill Trenary moved up to fourth place overall, also feeling flulike symptoms.

And Thomas? She finished third, behind Witt and the surprising Manley. After two-footing the landing of a triple combination jump shortly into

Elizabeth Manley gave one of the most enthusiastic Olympic performances ever seen.

Now a doctor, Debi Thomas made a run for Olympic gold while a full-time pre-med student.

her long program, she admitted, "I just didn't want to be out there anymore." Concentration shattered, she two-footed another triple landing and put her hand down on yet another.

At Worlds a few weeks later, the 1-2-3 results were identical, except now Thomas was married. Even her coach didn't know she had gotten married until someone from the media told him. Considering that Thomas should have kept her concentration focused entirely on skating during that crucial period, getting married just before Worlds was probably not what any coach would recommend. But then, maybe she figured after the Olympics that she couldn't really shatter her dream any further.

As a pro, Witt continued her unique way of toying with the audience and making viewers melt in the palm of her hand. While she was in Chicago with Brian Boitano's *Skating II* tour, a man with a camera yelled out to her as she passed by him in the front row. "Let me take your picture, Katarina," he begged. Normally, skaters would consider such a request as nothing more than an unwanted distraction that could break their focus. Witt, however, immediately altered her program, with the music still playing, and spent about half a minute posing for the surprised shutterbug.

The easing of East German travel restrictions in November 1989 should have been nothing but good news for Witt, who could now do exactly what she wanted, when she wanted. She had been allowed substantially more freedom than the average East German, but, frankly, she was not an "average" East German. She was considered by some of her fellow Germans to be far too friendly with the totalitarian regime that oppressed them, denying them the same travel freedoms that she enjoyed. When she went back home to the former East Germany to appear at a youth rally, she was, to her surprise, emphatically booed and called nasty names.

It seemed such an unexpected and unfortunate happening for someone so beloved outside of her own country. For a moment, at least, perhaps Witt was able to relate to the post–World War II home country reception received by the only other woman to win back-to-back Olympic figure skating titles, Sonja Henie.

Other 1980s Ladies

Debi Thomas enjoyed a substantial professional career after the 1988 Winter Olympics, while holding down a full load of university pre-med classes. She retired from competitions to devote all her time to medical studies. In 1997, she became Dr. Thomas and began her residency program with the goal of eventually practicing orthopedic surgery.

Jill Trenary won the 1987, 1989, and 1990 U.S. Nationals, placing second in 1988 to Thomas. She continually moved up in the world rankings, eventually placing first in 1990 and winning the compulsory figures event the last time it would be held at Worlds. Her fourth-place finish at the 1988 Winter Olympics set her up as a possible medalist in 1992, but she sprained an ankle at the 1991 U.S. Nationals and pulled out of the competition, turning pro as the defending World Champion. This meant she gave up her shot at the

Jill Trenary was equally adept at free skating and performing the once-compulsory figures.

1992 Winter Olympics, the last Olympics not to allow professionals to reinstate.

Because figures played a part in her victory, she is considered by some to be the last "total" Ladies' Champion. Now married to Christopher Dean, she has a much more relaxed feeling about being on the ice, stating, "I realize now that if I don't hit a triple, the program can still be very, very good. It's a matter of focusing more on the entire package, including the costuming and expressions. What happens between *A* and Z is more important than what happened at, let's say, D." Recognizing the difference between amateur competition and professional exhibitions, she adds, "Of course, I wouldn't have achieved becoming World Champion in 1990 if I had this attitude then."

In 1988, Japanese spark plug Midori Ito became the first Ladies' competitor to pull off a triple axel in competition. She won the 1989 Worlds and then placed second to Trenary at the 1990 Worlds. Her 1989 performance was notable for a dazzling display of jumping that, because of her small stature, seemed to propel her into the air like a missile. And she continually wore a genuine smile that lit up the Paris arena.

At the 1991 Worlds, she jumped right through the hole in the rink wall where a TV camera was sitting. Despite this, she was considered a favorite to win the 1992 Winter Olympics in Albertville, France, but she finished second to Kristi Yamaguchi, amidst an avalanche of Japanese media coverage that put a phenomenal amount of pressure on her. Plus, her concentration was totally shattered by French skater Surya Bonaly, who did a back flip—an illegal move in amateur competition—right in front of her while she was getting ready to set up her own jump during the long program warm-up session.

Midori Ito remains the most famous figure skater to come out of Japan.

Ito is regarded as perhaps the most gracious skater ever to have been on the ice. After her encounter with the wall in 1991, she skated over to the gaping hole to apologize to the cameraman and to pick up pieces of wall that had fallen on the ice. And after her "disappointing" Olympic finish in 1992, she went on Japanese television to apologize to all her countryfolk, whom she felt she had let down.

Elaine Zayak, discussed in an earlier chapter, disappeared for some time, then reinstated her eligibility for the 1994 U.S. Championships. She finished an admirable fourth, having made clear all along that even if she qualified for the Olympics, she would not go. She entered the competition only for personal satisfaction and would not consider "depriving" an amateur skater of being selected for the World and Olympic Team.

Tiffany Chin won the bronze medal at the 1983 and 1986 U.S. Nationals, the silver in 1984, and the gold in 1985. She showed great promise by taking fourth place at the 1984 Winter Olympics, with many feeling that she should have taken the bronze of Soviet Kira Ivanova, a lackluster free skater but more solid in the figures than Chin. She went on to take World bronze in 1985 and 1986, then seemed to burn out. She skates today as a solo and ensemble performer in touring professional ice shows.

Denise Biellmann, 1981 World Champion, has had a phenomenal professional career. Continuing to stretch the athletic and artistic envelopes (as well as her leg during her trademark Biellmann Spin), she's won numerous contests over skaters many years her junior. Her programs occasionally are a bit experimental for some tastes, but she continues to push forward, taking the risk that the audience might not understand her as well as the judges.

Other 1980s Men

David Santee started off the decade with much potential for the future, placing fourth at the 1980 Winter Olympics and Worlds. In 1981, only Scott Hamilton stood between him and the gold medal at Worlds, his one and only time on the Worlds medals podium.

Santee came from a skating family; his brother James also made some impressions at Nationals, although he never appeared on the

Working with John Curry's ice ballet company revealed David Santee's hidden artistry.

podium. David Santee was perhaps best known for his semiportrayal of Rocky Balboa from the Sylvester Stallone hit film *Rocky*. After a while, though, it seemed as if he were stalled artistically, and he left amateur competition. Many were surprised when he signed on to skate with John Curry's ice ballet company, but the change did him a world of good and allowed him to discover his artistic inner soul.

Czechoslovakian skater Jozef Sabovcik was a surprise bronze medalist at the 1984 Winter Olympics, as he had no medals from prior Worlds. Because he was sixth at the 1983 Worlds, he felt no pressure at the Olympics. He remembers, "My teammates and I were always worried about our hockey players, and the skiers all had tremendous problems with the snow. I was watching all the other events, and suddenly it was time for me to go and perform and I didn't have any time to dread it. The incredible thing was I ended up with a medal I didn't expect."

He had severe difficulties with his legs and was told by many people to skip the Olympics because his knees might "blow out." However, he had missed a chance to go to the 1980 Winter Olympics in Lake Placid because the Czech skating federation didn't have the money to send any athletes, so he wasn't about to miss out on Sarajevo. He

Jozef Sabovcik has earned the nickname Jumpin' Joe for his huge, dazzling jumps.

says he was taking off his skates after his Olympic long program when someone ran in and yelled that he had come in third. He didn't even realize that meant he had to go out to the podium until it was suggested he should go out to the rink to pick up his medal.

His knees did prevent him from contending in future years. In 1986, he was in second place going into the long program at Worlds, but then his knee acted up. Every landing left him visibly in pain, and by the end of the program, he could barely stand.

A while later, he left Czechoslovakia for Canada, where he became associated with Toller Cranston, saying Cranston doesn't care as much about where the jumps go as he wants him to understand "what is that music trying to portray and what is it trying to tell me?"

At the 1986 European Championships, Sabovcik was the first to stand up on a quad jump, but a mistake on the landing meant that Kurt Browning would get the credit for successfully landing the first quad in international competition. Lately, Sabovcik has enjoyed a competitive rebirth because of all the professional competitions now being held. He is always a threat and has won a number of events, still knocking off big jumps, including quads. This has earned him the respect of fellow skaters and the nickname Jumpin' Joe.

Christopher Bowman was a skater who promised to be one of the biggest names ever. Naturally talented and blessed with a Hollywood flair for the dramatic, he captivated audiences and loved playing to the fans, the judges, and the cameras. He was as much a free spirit as his coach, Frank Carroll, was not. Carroll often tried to get Bowman to focus on disciplining himself, but with all that natural talent and success, Bowman didn't see much reason not to have as much fun as he could along the way, playing up his party image whenever he could.

He first came to the public eye as a baby in television commercials, so the showmanship was practically bred into him. He was called Bowman the Showman by admirers and detractors alike, and he did nothing to discourage the nickname.

Christopher
Bowman was
known as
Bowman the
Showman.

He twice took the silver medal and twice took the bronze at the U.S. Nationals, and he won the gold in 1989. His placements at Worlds from 1987 through 1991 were seventh, fifth, second, third, and fourth. He was seventh in the 1988 Winter Olympics and fourth in 1992, edged for a medal by Czechoslovakian Petr Barna.

He had many run-ins with coach Carroll, but none more publicly than after his 1990 Worlds long program. Carroll had tried to teach Bowman personal responsibility (Bowman referred to himself as Hans Brinker from Hell) and was infuriated when Bowman, after a shaky start, totally rechoreographed his long program as he skated it. Carroll recognized nothing of what the two had worked on for months. When he pointed this out to Bowman after he got off the ice, Bowman insulted Carroll by responding, "All head and no heart." They then went to the "kiss and cry" area to await the scores. Bowman was ecstatic with the high marks that earned him a Worlds bronze medal, but it was clear to everyone watching on TV that Carroll was anything but amused. It was the beginning of the end of their relationship.

Later, Bowman went to study under Toller Cranston, a totally different personality and one who emphasized a balletic approach to choreography. Cranston, when asked how he was going to package Bowman, announced he was going to "dip him in black." And so he attired Bowman in a dignified, solid black costume, turning Bowman into a younger version of himself. Bowman looked very, very uncomfortable with his new, less showy image.

Bowman then made some personal decisions that would haunt him for some time, but he eventually recovered from his lapses to become a respected TV commentator of skating competitions. But there are still some fans, remembering his potential, who wonder what would have happened had his ability to focus on the end result been equal to his natural gifts.

Alexandr Fadeev of the Soviet Union tried for a quad toe loop at the 1986 Worlds but didn't get credit for being the first because it

Alexandr Fadeev was one of the best Men's skaters to come out of the former Soviet Union.

wasn't executed perfectly. In fact, he failed spectacularly, but in doing so he threw down the gauntlet, and other skaters would know that if it could be attempted, it could be achieved. He won the bronze medal at Worlds in 1984, 1986, and 1987 and won Worlds in 1985 with a dizzying performance that left him sweating and looking totally exhausted at the end.

In 1986, he felt pressured to try the quad. What happened next was enough to make him want to crawl under the ice and hide. He fell out of two triples, touched his hand to the ice on another, and over-rotated yet another. The quad was a total disaster. He received dismal marks of 5.4 to 5.6, which should have knocked him off the medals stand altogether. However, the Soviet judge saw fit to award him two marks of 5.8 and 5.9, as if nothing bad had happened. The audience in Switzerland booed loudly, and this obvious act of nationalism went down as one of the most blatant and scandalous ever.

While Fadeev and Sabovcik tried mightily to be the first to get credit for landing a quad jump in international competition, Canadian Champion Kurt Browning is in the record books as the man who did achieve where others failed. He accomplished this feat at the 1988 Worlds, in which—because of the figures—he finished sixth overall (behind Champion Brian Boitano) despite taking third place in the long program.

However, Browning did win the next three Worlds and placed second to Viktor Petrenko in 1992, returning to win the 1993 Worlds over up-and-coming teammate Elvis Stojko. Despite going on to take the silver medal at the 1992 Worlds a few weeks later, he had a devastating time at the 1992 Winter Olympics in Albertville, placing sixth. All his fans felt that he truly deserved better, considering his remarkable achievements up to that time, but in figure skating, despite occasional judging irregularities, you typically get only what you deserve at the moment.

Kurt Browning performed the first quad in international competition.

part

Skating Turned Upside Down

Pre-Lillehammer

IT SEEMS THAT EVERYTHING THAT HAPPENED IN SKATING in the early 1990s was largely overshadowed by the events of 1994. And yet, some very fine skating took place in the years leading up to the reinstatement of professionals and the bizarre Harding/Kerrigan affair.

Lost in the madness of the 1994 Winter Olympics was the fact that just two years earlier, there was another Winter Olympics, in Albertville, France, the last to be held in the same year as the Summer Olympics.

A few personalities of the early 1990s were discussed in previous chapters, crossing over from the 1980s. Some of those, plus others who didn't become big names until the early 1990s, were Soviets who found that by 1992, the country they used to represent no longer existed.

Viktor Petrenko, World and Olympic bronze medalist in 1988, World silver medalist in 1990 and 1991, and World and Olympic gold medalist in 1992, skated most of his amateur career as a Soviet but was proud to declare himself a Ukrainian in 1992, when the USSR broke up just before the Winter Olympics. However, Ukraine wasn't recognized as an ISU member until 1993, so, in 1992, he and other former Soviets skated under the banner of a country that didn't really exist, the Commonwealth of Independent States.

Petrenko turned pro after his Olympic victory, but he didn't really enjoy it. For one thing, there was a limited number of professional competitions then, and he missed the thrill of competing. He jumped at the chance to reinstate as an amateur for the 1994 Winter Olympics. He won many events as a second-time amateur,

Olympic gold
medalist Viktor
Petrenko

but a mistake in the Olympic short program put him in ninth going into the free skate, killing his chances of earning a medal. With a strong long program, he moved up to fourth.

As a successful professional who reinstated as an amateur singles skater, Petrenko wasn't alone in not living up to past potential during the 1994 Olympics. The Winter Games were not kind to Brian Boitano or Katarina Witt either.

Many thought that American Paul Wylie's silver medal performance in the 1992 Winter Olympics was worthy of the gold. From 1988 through 1992, he alternated between second and third place at the USFSA Nationals, never managing to win. In the three years he was sent to Worlds, he placed ninth, tenth, and eleventh. In 1992, he was chosen for the U.S. Olympic Team, but not to go to the Worlds. Perhaps that's why judges had a little difficulty dealing with his being so "on" in Albertville.

Wylie relishes his expressive dynamism, enjoying skating to programs that tell a story. He was always popular with the audiences as an amateur but just couldn't pull it together to achieve his potential until Albertville. His coach blamed that on his habit of thinking too

Paul Wylie astounded everyone by almost winning Olympic gold at Albertville, France.

Enjoying success in singles and Pairs, Kristi Yamaguchi decided to concentrate solely on singles and went straight to the highest step of the Olympic podium.

much about everything he did. One of the brightest people ever to strap on a pair of skates, he found it difficult to skate with abandon.

After his stellar Olympic performance, he turned pro and had a spectacular pro career, finishing it up in 1998, still in his prime, in order to return to Harvard and pursue a degree in law.

Kristi Yamaguchi was the big story in early 1990s Ladies' skating, placing second at the USFSA Nationals in 1989, 1990, and 1991, winning Worlds in 1991, and winning Nationals, Worlds, and the Winter Olympics in 1992, over Midori Ito and a rising Nancy Kerrigan.

As a five-year-old, Yamaguchi used to skate around her rink while clutching a Dorothy Hamill doll, having taken up the sport because the 1976 Olympic Champion was her idol.

For a while, she excelled in both singles and Pairs skating. In 1989 and 1990, she won the USFSA Pairs Championship with partner Rudy Galindo. Both years they placed fifth at Worlds. However, she suspected that her chances of medaling in Pairs at Worlds or the Olympics were fairly remote, as the Soviet Pairs skaters were so strong. After the 1990 USFSA Pairs victory, she broke up with Galindo and concentrated solely on singles skating. It must have worked, because she went straight to the top the next two years. Galindo became a singles skater as well, struggling competitively and financially until his stunning USFSA Championship performance in 1996.

Yamaguchi has enjoyed an outstanding professional career since turning pro in 1992, excelling in programs that are of a carefree nature.

Natalia Mishkutenok and Artur Dmitriev were products of supercoach Tamara Moskvina. They

No Pairs skater had more flexibility than Natalia Mishkutenok, shown with partner Artur Dmitriev.

placed third at the 1990 Worlds and then won Worlds in 1991 and 1992, also winning the 1992 Winter Olympics. Perhaps no Pairs team since Belousova and Protopopov in the mid-1960s has been more poetic. They were famous for unique spins that flaunted her flexibility—especially their trademark spin wherein she hugged close to his legs while upside down.

After 1992, the team experienced difficulties in keeping their partnership together. They all but disappeared in 1993 and came back for the 1994 Winter Olympics, holding their relationship together by a thread. They performed spectacularly, and some thought they could have beaten Gordeeva and Grinkov. However, they weren't quite as polished as their Russian teammates, though they were dripping with emotion.

After the 1994 Winter Olympics, Dmitriev paired up with Oksana

With Oksana Kazakova, Artur Dmitriev won his second Olympic gold medal.

Kazakova, moving up through the ranks to win the 1998 Winter Olympics. Dmitriev is outspoken about the restrictions of Pairs skating, stating, "We must do three lifts, two throws, three jumps, two spins, two death spirals, and steps. I think we must add more difficulty. If you talk about elements and compare today [1997] to the 1984 Olympic Games, it's the same difficulty level. The same throws, the same jumps, the same twists."

Blurring the Line between Amateurs and Professionals

It had always been accepted that once skaters had a chance to turn professional, they would cheerfully leave the world of amateur skating and enter their postcompetitive days, where they could make money. Before skating became the popular sensation it is today, turning pro often meant signing on with a big tour such as *Ice Capades, Ice Follies,* and *Holiday on Ice.* Only a few skaters became marquee names that attracted paying audience members. Many more became members of the chorus—the ensemble that skated to big, glitzy musical numbers and wore extravagant costumes.

It was easy to know who was an amateur and who was a pro. Amateurs competed—pros didn't. Amateurs didn't make money— pros did. (Under the old ISU rules, amateurs couldn't even make money performing in exhibitions, although trust funds to help defer training expenses were common.)

Dick Button started to change the equation when he held the first big, nationally televised professional competition in 1980, now known as the NutraSweet World Professional Figure Skating Championship. The event gave pros a chance to rediscover the joys of competition, with fewer restrictions than were found in ISU-sanctioned events. (For example, pros could skate to music with words. Amateurs could do so only in exhibitions.) Button's professional competitions required two separate full-length programs, one emphasizing technical proficiency and the other artistry.

After his win at the 1988 Winter Olympics, Brian Boitano entered and won an incredible string of professional competitions, continuing to improve his technique and artistry to the point where no other male skater could catch him. If he for some reason hadn't turned pro, he could have won the 1992 Winter Olympics. And this possibility disturbed him greatly. He became quite vocal that the Olympics should be open to the best athletes in the world, regardless of their amateur or professional status. Boitano pointed out that in many other Olympic sports, professionals were allowed to compete. Certainly the top skiers made a lot of money from endorsements and commercials, as did top summer sports athletes such as track and basketball stars. If Michael Jordan was allowed to play on America's Dream Team, why should Brian Boitano be barred from competing in the most prestigious athletic event in the world?

In 1991, the International Skating Union issued guidelines to allow amateur skaters to receive pay from competitions, exhibitions, and endorsements, yet still remain eligible to compete in ISU events. The catch was that the events had to be sanctioned by the ISU and the funds had to go through the skaters' national governing bodies. However, the ISU still did not allow for professionals to reinstate as amateurs. But allowing amateurs to make money was the first step in cracking the door open for professionals to come back some year into the ISU fold.

After years of considering the possibility and rejecting it, the ISU finally decided that pros could reinstate for the 1994 Winter Olympics, in essence allowing them to reenter the ranks of amateur skating. There was quite a bit of controversy over this decision, with many pointing out that the top pros could end up taking away spots from deserving amateurs who had patiently waited for their chance to go to the Olympics. The ruling allowing professionals to come back to the Olympics became commonly known as the Boitano Rule. Not everyone used the term with endearment.

Many thought that Boitano would be somewhat lonely on the ice, surmising that pros would not want to take the time to train hard to get back into the kind of physical and mental condition necessary for intense amateur competition. But when it came time for pro skaters to announce their intentions to reinstate, Boitano was joined by a number of former Olympic gold medalists, including Viktor Petrenko, Katarina Witt, the Ice Dancing team of Jayne Torvill and Christopher Dean, the Pairs team of Ekaterina Gordeeva and Sergei Grinkov, and the Pairs team of Natalia Mishkutenok and Artur Dmitriev. Elaine Zayak also reinstated, for the USFSA Championships only. Unlike the others, she had no desire to reenter the world stage.

When the dust settled after the 1994 Winter Olympics in Lillehammer, Norway, the professionals who had reinstated went home with mixed results. Gordeeva and Grinkov won their second Olympic gold medal for Pairs, followed by a reenergized Mishkutenok and Dmitriev. Petrenko, Boitano, and four-time World Champion Kurt Browning (still an amateur) experienced calamities that destroyed their medal hopes—falls that almost never plagued them any other time. Browning had hoped to get the Olympic medal that eluded him in 1992.

Like the reinstated Men, Witt also finished out of medal placement, but was never really considered a front-runner to begin with. Hers was more of a personal victory. Her parents had not been allowed to travel out of East Germany to see her win her previous two Olympic gold medals, having to contend with severe travel restrictions placed upon them by a government always fearful of the possibility of embarrassing defections. In Lillehammer, with Germany reunified and the people now free, Witt's parents were finally able to see her skate live in the Winter Olympics.

Torvill and Dean finished third in Ice Dancing, despite overwhelming public sentiment that they were still the best. Ten years after winning the Olympic gold, with *Bolero* still fresh in skating fans' minds, they returned to the amateur scene with a more traditional *Face the Music* program. They realized that in some ways the world of Ice Dancing had moved backward since 1984. They won the European Championship but were told by judges that they weren't "dancing" enough for the rules of 1994. Taking the advice to heart, they changed more than half their program for the Olympics a few weeks later and were beaten by two teams they had defeated at the Europeans.

Harding's Fall from Grace

The reinstatement of professionals was *supposed* to be the big story at the 1994 Winter Olympics, the first Winter Games to be held in a year apart from the Summer Olympics. And then a strange little incident in Detroit, Michigan, changed all that.

Tonya Harding was talented enough to have it all. She was the first American woman to pull off a successful three-and-a-half-revolution triple axel in competition and only the second woman (after Midori Ito) in the world to do one. She was an up-and-coming skater when she won the bronze medal at the 1989 USFSA Championships, but she had a rough year in 1990. She then came back and stunned the skating world by winning Nationals in 1991, defeating eventual 1992 Winter Olympic Champion Kristi Yamaguchi and the person with whom she would become forever connected in the public's eye, Nancy Kerrigan. In 1991, Yamaguchi defeated her at Worlds, but Harding stood on the Worlds medals stand with bronze medalist Kerrigan, for a 1-2-3 American Ladies' medals sweep and what would be her only trip to the podium.

The American public was quite fond of Harding. She was poor. She had had a rough childhood. She trained in a public rink in the wide-open atrium of an indoor shopping center outside Portland, Oregon. She drove a pickup truck. She had real faults and didn't attempt to hide them. Despite suffering from asthma, she smoked cigarettes. She was a fighter—literally. A well-publicized traffic confrontation found her going after another motorist with a baseball bat. Harding was anything but a prim and proper skating icon. She was real, and gritty, and didn't fit in the mold of a traditional skating princess. She was the common person, the underdog, the skater whom parents didn't want their sons to bring home, but the skater with whom the sons were probably most intrigued.

In 1992, Harding took the bronze at Nationals and almost got a medal at the Albertville, France, Winter Olympics. Her trademark triple axel betrayed her in the short program, and she ended up in fourth after the long program. A sixth-place finish at Worlds a few weeks later was the beginning of the slide downward that kept her off the USFSA medals stand in 1993. But her husband, Jeff Gillooly, would eventually formulate a plan to assure that no one would stand in her way in 1994.

Thursday, January 6, 1994, became a day that will live in infamy.

Gillooly had a couple of friends with whom he shared his plan: to take Nancy Kerrigan out of the USFSA Nationals competition in Detroit. One of these friends somehow sneaked backstage after Kerrigan completed a practice session prior to the beginning of the Ladies' competition. In the hallway Kerrigan was passing through, he whacked her hard on her right knee with a collapsible police baton, crippling Kerrigan instantly. He then ran down the hallway, crashed through a window, and disappeared into a waiting escape car.

A handheld video camera was soon on the scene, catching Kerrigan's anguished cries of "Why me?" while she lay on the floor of the hallway in pain. With a chance to win the upcoming Winter Olympics seemingly dashed in an instant of brutal ferocity, she thought everything she had worked for had been taken from her by an act she could not comprehend.

It turned out that Kerrigan's knee wasn't broken, but it was severely bruised and would keep her from defending her 1993

Tonya Harding was known by many as skating's "bad girl."

Nationals title. Harding issued a lukewarm "best wishes" to Kerrigan and went on to win the 1994 USFSA Ladies' title as if she knew nothing about the incident. Kerrigan watched the long program in person, as suspicions started to mount that Harding was somehow involved in the madness.

Because of heavy news coverage of the attack, television viewership of Nationals was high. A USFSA committee soon voted to send Kerrigan to the Olympics, if she recovered in time to compete. Harding was to be sent, too, because it was not yet clear if she'd had any involvement. Michelle Kwan was to be sent as an alternate in case Kerrigan couldn't skate. Because Kerrigan was the only U.S. skater to place in the top ten at the previous year's Worlds, the country was allowed only two Ladies' skaters for the 1994 Olympics and Worlds.

The Winter Olympics Ladies' competition was just seven weeks later in Lillehammer. During that time, Kerrigan went through an astounding training regimen to get back on the ice. As she remembers, "I never worked so hard in my life." It took every ounce of strength she had to try to pull herself back into shape.

Meanwhile, investigators started to close the noose around Harding. Too many things didn't add up. New details appeared nightly on the national networks about what had probably happened. In a short time, the public became convinced that Harding had had something to do with the attack. The USFSA became convinced as well.

Realizing this, Harding took legal action to prevent the USFSA from keeping her out of the Olympics until her role in the attack, if any, was determined beyond a shadow of a doubt. She filed a $25 million lawsuit against the USFSA to prevent it from taking her off the Olympic team. She continued to train as if nothing was wrong, but the TV cameras that flooded the sides of her training rink were enough to let anyone know that the media smelled a hot story and weren't going to miss any of it.

By the time of the Olympics, Harding had been found guilty in the court of public opinion. She stayed away from Norway until the last possible moment, and when she appeared in Lillehammer, the cameras followed her every move. They also focused on Nancy Kerrigan, whose training/rehabilitation regimen had paid off. She was determined to show the world that memories of the attack would not keep her down.

The Ladies' short program from Lillehammer garnered huge television ratings. But it was the long program where the twisted story set new standards for bizarreness. Harding botched a jump early in her program and then suddenly stopped skating. She went over to the judges, crying, showing them that her boot lace had broken. The television commentator said it was a ploy he had seen her use before when she wasn't skating well at the start of a program. No one in her entourage had a spare lace immediately available. She would have to start the program over, but it did not help her. Harding, who had tried to keep the world from caving in on her since the Detroit attack, would finish eighth.

Kerrigan skated brilliantly and was first after the short program. She presented a very fine long program but lost the gold medal by the scantiest of margins. She was placed first by the four judges from the Western countries and was placed second by

Heroically fighting back from a vicious attack on her knee, Nancy Kerrigan won Olympic silver.

four judges from the Eastern countries. Jan Hoffman, the German judge and former Men's World Champion, tied Kerrigan and Oksana Baiul. But he gave Kerrigan a 5.8 in Artistic Impression and Baiul a 5.9. That .1 was the entire tie-breaking margin of victory for Baiul, even though she had two-footed a landing on one of her jumps.

In all the media publicity over the Harding/Kerrigan matchup, defending World Champion Oksana Baiul had almost been lost in the shuffle. She trained in Lillehammer in relative seclusion and took the ice feeling little of the pressure felt by Harding and Kerrigan. And when it was over, with Harding in eighth, there really was no Harding/Kerrigan matchup, after all.

Ukrainian Baiul had come out of nowhere the year before to win the 1993 Worlds at the age of fifteen. In 1992, she wasn't even one of the top ten skaters in the transitional former Soviet Union. Orphaned at an early age, she was supported by 1992 Olympic gold medalist Viktor Petrenko out of the fees he earned as a professional. She moved in with his coach and mother-in-law, Galina Zmievskaya, who became a surrogate mother to her and would work on-ice wonders with her in a short time.

Her expressive artistry was beyond compare, and so was her resolve. The day after a serious collision with another skater in an Olympics practice session, she skated in pain with stitches in her leg. And, after missing a triple in the Olympics long program, she threw another one in toward the end. That, and skating on her cut leg, showed she was as gutsy a performer as Kerrigan, who, at twenty-four, was eight years her senior.

It almost seemed an anticlimax to the Olympics that Kerrigan didn't win. With a silver medal, Kerrigan went on to do many product endorsements and was identified by American Sports Data in 1996 as the number one most-recognized female athlete in America. Plus, Disney signed her to a variety of projects.

And Harding? Well, she became the closest thing the skating world has to a nonperson. Her husband, who soon became her ex-

Oksana Baiul came out of total obscurity to win the World Championship and the 1994 Winter Olympics.

husband, and his two friends were found guilty of planning the attack on Kerrigan and spent time in prison for their crimes. When it was confirmed that Harding had indeed known about the attack and had lied about it to authorities, she was sentenced to perform hundreds of hours of community service and received massive monetary fines.

In June 1994, a USFSA Hearing Panel stripped Harding of her ill-won Ladies' title as punishment for her involvement in the attack. Three months later, the USFSA Executive Committee voted to leave the title vacant, the only time this has ever happened. Officially, there is no USFSA Ladies' Champion for 1994. She was also banned for life from ever competing as an amateur.

She could, however, perform as a professional. But it is virtually certain that this will never happen. While she would sell a lot of tickets, many professional skaters are said to have "Tonya clauses" in their contracts with ice shows and competitions. If she's in, they're out.

It was an unfortunate end to what was one of the most promising careers in all of skating.

Post-Lillehammer Ladies

Japan's Yuka Sato was born to parents who both were Japanese Champions and had represented Japan at the Winter Olympics. A few weeks after Lillehammer, she turned the tables on France's Surya Bonaly at the 1994 Worlds, held in Japan. The competitive field was smaller than at Lillehammer, as is often the case in an Olympic year, with the three Olympic medalists out of the picture. Baiul and Kerrigan had already turned pro, and Lu Chen, Olympic bronze medalist from China, went home to take care of a nagging foot problem.

Bonaly captured the silver medal at three Worlds in a row—1993, 1994, and 1995. She fully expected to win the 1994 event, and at the medal ceremony in Japan, she shocked the skating world by removing her medal from around her neck after it had been presented, holding it in her hand while the Japanese national anthem was played. Considering that the World Championships were in Japan, this created an even bigger stir. Realizing her mistake, she publicly apologized to the Japanese people for her action.

The Japanese people remembered that Bonaly was the skater who threw off Midori Ito's concentration at the 1992 Winter Olympics by doing a back flip in front of her while Ito was setting up a jump in warm-up for the long program. There was little reason for Bonaly, an accomplished gymnast, to try such a jump. Back flips are illegal in amateur competition because the move allegedly cannot be landed on one foot, which is a requirement of all jumps. But in 1994, in the Lillehammer exhibition, where rules are less restrictive, Bonaly not only nailed a back flip but astounded everyone by landing it on one foot. No one else, including all the men who perform it regularly in professional competition, has the incredible strength to do likewise.

Surya Bonaly is the first Ladies' skater to successfully perform a quad.

Bonaly has a strong opinion about the rule forbidding back flips in amateur competition, stating, "It's stupid. I've done it on one foot, and I can do it in combination with a triple jump—a triple salchow on the same foot right away after the back flip." Although other women have done back flips, she is the only person to do one in a split position, with the legs split. Most men who can do a back flip are afraid to try that one.

She is the only Ladies' skater who can pull off a quad jump, and she actually attempted one in the 1992 Winter Olympics. More impressively, she can do two quads—a salchow and a toe loop— and has pulled them off in exhibitions. But her dedication to jumping comes at a price, as she has long been criticized for not devoting enough time to working on artistry.

Bonaly finds the rules for singles skaters to be too restrictive. Her mother, Suzanne, points out, "Skating is the only sport where the rules state, 'You must not do more than this.' It's like being in jail. The rules are like a ceiling. She can do so much, but the rules are holding her back. I think everyone in the public loses, as they don't get a chance to see what can be done."

Lu Chen returned to competition after her foot healed to win the 1995 Worlds over Bonaly and the United States' Nicole Bobek. As big as China is, Chen says there may be fewer than ten rinks in the entire country, so she had no skating tradition to draw on. In 1996, she delivered a breathtaking long program at Worlds, earning some perfect scores of 6.0. Many would have given her another gold medal on the spot, but the United States' Michelle Kwan came out on the ice and earned even more perfect scores. Kwan raised the stakes in the long program by throwing in an extra triple toe at the end of her program, a move that could have knocked her off the medals stand had she failed. Her perfection was enough to beat Chen's perfection. It was a competition where a tie that couldn't have been broken would have been an appropriate solution.

Kwan had had a lot of pressure on her at the 1994 Worlds. With Kerrigan and Harding out of the picture, the thirteen-year-old Olympic alternate was on her own, attempting to salvage two positions for the United States for the 1995 Worlds. To do so, she would have to place among the top ten Ladies' skaters. Additional pressure was thrust upon her when Nicole Bobek fell apart miserably in the qualification round, placing thirteenth in her group. Kwan showed what a fighter she was by finishing in eighth place, and, as a result, she salvaged her own second-place position on the World Team for the next year.

Kwan doesn't worry as much as most other skaters about missing jumps. According to her choreographer, Lori Nichol, "She doesn't get really upset if she misses something. It's just a fact, it's just something that happens, and she'll fix it next time. So nothing ever really gets her down or really gets her too up. She was excited after [1996] Worlds. She kept pinching herself, [asking,] 'Is this real?' And within fifteen minutes, she was talking about the sunglasses she wanted to go buy. So in that fifteen minutes, we were back to reality."

Tara Lipinski made many sacrifices in her quest for the gold. She moved to Detroit to train with her coach, while her father stayed behind in Texas to work and raise money for her training expenses. It's not uncommon for a world-level skater to spend more than $50,000 per year for training, equipment, travel, and other incidentals. The Lipinski family had to take out a second mortgage on their house to pay for her expenses. But the result was worth it—a World Championship and a Winter Olympics crown.

With fluid movement and seamless choreography, Michelle Kwan is the epitome of sophisticated elegance.

Lipinski won her first USFSA Nationals medal, a bronze, in 1996. One year later she was National and World Champion at the age of fourteen, the youngest World Champion ever, just a few months younger than Sonja Henie had been when she won her first Worlds in 1927. Interestingly, she would not have even qualified to go to Worlds in 1997 under the ISU's new age limit policy, instituted to assure that participants at Worlds would be at least fifteen years old. Lipinski was "grand-

fathered" in because she had competed at Worlds the year before.

The reason for such a ruling was to protect the young skaters. The ISU didn't want younger skaters to feel obligated to try some of the maneuvers they would need in order to compete on the world level. The risk of injury to extremely young skaters attempting world-class-level jumps was deemed too great.

While male skaters have to mature to be able to perfect the more explosive jumps, female skaters find it easier to toss off the jumps while they are younger. Males don't have the necessary muscle masses until they're a bit older. Females find that once they have gone through puberty, their center of gravity has changed, and in many cases, they have to learn to jump all over again. There have been many cases in which a Ladies' skater achieved success at a very early age, ran into roadblocks during puberty, and then slowly came back to competitive form afterward.

The discrepancy between age and success for Ladies and Men at Worlds is clear when one looks at the record books. The youngest Ladies' World Champion was Lipinski, at age fourteen. The youngest Men's World Champion was Donald McPherson of Canada, who was eighteen when he won in 1963.

Jill Trenary is concerned about the trend to younger Ladies' skaters, but for reasons of personal—rather than physical—development. She says, "It's hard for me to see some girls being out of school at fifteen or sixteen. They're doing nothing but skating, but I think being in school is important to being a total person. Some of these girls are missing out on having a real life. Hopefully they'll have a strong upbringing that can help them through it all.

"I'm concerned about seeing many young girls achieving fame and glory so soon while they're so young. I hate to say it, but the money that comes with such an early success is not necessarily a good thing. I just hope they stay close to their families and skate because they love skating and not because they're hooked on the TV coverage or money. I hope they do it for themselves."

At fifteen, Tara Lipinski was the youngest Olympic gold medalist in history.

After winning the 1995 USFSA Championship and capturing the bronze medal at Worlds that year, Nicole Bobek had a really rough 1996 and wasn't sent to Worlds after she pulled out of Nationals with an injury. There was precedent to send her, as the USFSA had done so in the past with other skaters who were temporarily injured. Her Worlds medal the year before was in her favor, but in the end, a committee decided to send third-place Lipinski instead.

Some felt that the USFSA was punishing Bobek for not training hard enough heading into Nationals. She participated with teammate Todd Eldredge as a featured skater in *Nutcracker on Ice,* just a month prior to Nationals. The press was merciless about the appearance that both skaters were taking Nationals for granted.

Bobek has long been misunderstood by the mainstream press. She's a free spirit who at times seems to enjoy poking fun at established conventions. The media have interpreted this as meaning that she doesn't care about competing, which is far from the truth. She cares, but she wants to enjoy herself along the way. She has received very little attention for her ongoing work with Touch the Heart and Raise the Spirit, where she goes into elementary schools and talks to students about what it took to achieve success.

The media enjoyed picking on the fact that she has had more than her share of coaches. She would have stuck with the great Carlo Fassi had he not moved back to Italy. Things just weren't right with some of her other coaches, and she longed

Nicole Bobek's training regimen and numerous coaching changes were sometimes frowned upon by the USFSA.

for Fassi. They were able to get together once again for the 1997 season, and through working with him she was able to reclaim a spot on the World Team, behind Lipinski and Kwan. Then, at Worlds in Lausanne, Switzerland, the unthinkable happened. Fassi died of a sudden heart attack. Bobek came unglued in the short program and got her emotional strength together for the long program. At the end, she went to her knees and gave a silent prayer in his memory. It was one of the most touching moments ever witnessed on the ice.

Post-Lillehammer Men

Many thought the dissolution of the Soviet Union in 1992 would negatively affect the development of top skaters there. This was not the case at the 1994 Winter Olympics, as all the gold medalists came from either Russia (Urmanov, Gordeeva and Grinkov, and Grishuk and Platov) or Ukraine (Baiul).

Alexei Urmanov was quite a surprise at the Olympics. He was first seen on the medals stand as bronze medalist at the 1993 Worlds, his last appearance on the Worlds podium. As the favored reinstated professionals fell by the wayside, he performed solidly, if not exactly with much spirit. But there was little to be found wrong with his performance, and his ended up being the best out of a lot of performances that were less than sterling.

Canada's Elvis Stojko attacked the Worlds scene with his unique training in the martial arts. He took the bronze in 1992, and the silver in 1993, and he won it all in 1994, 1995, and 1997, capturing Olympic silver in 1994. He had a rough time in the short program at the 1996 Worlds in Edmonton, Canada, dashing his hopes to win a medal in his home country with an uncharacteristic fall caused by over-rotating a triple axel. But he came back with one of the most startling long programs ever skated.

With the audience going berserk, he grabbed an *Edmonton Sun* newspaper that had come out after the short program and held it up to the cameras. The big headline, plastered across the front page over

Elvis Stojko's black belt training in martial arts inspires his skating.

a picture of the earlier fall, read ELVIS IS DEAD. Stojko comments, "It's so weird how one jump can make all the difference in the way people look at things. The most important thing in [the] sport is not if you fall, but how fast you get up and continue."

Stojko has the most consistent quad in the business, so pulling off triples is normally easy for him. But the fall that cost him a Worlds medal, and probably the gold as well, left him reflecting on the qualities that make him the great performer he is. He says, "Everything happens for a reason. If you go for it all the way and you don't quite make it, you're hungrier the next time, because you're going to do it next time."

Todd Eldredge has demonstrated his ability to fight back. After winning the 1990 and 1991 USFSA Men's Championship, he didn't even make it to the Nationals medals stand for the next three years. In 1995, he blasted back to win the gold and then lost to Rudy Galindo in 1996 when Galindo delivered the performance of several lifetimes in his hometown of San Jose, California. But Eldredge once again fought back and won the gold

Todd Eldredge has often fought back from adversity to achieve great success.

in 1997. He also won the Worlds bronze in 1991, the silver (behind Stojko) in 1995 and 1997, and the gold in 1996, coming back to best Galindo on the world stage.

He admits to being "burned out" in 1993, partially as a result of the back injury that plagued him the year before. He might have regained a spot on the World and Olympic Team in 1994 had he not come down with the flu at the U.S. Nationals, placing fourth.

One reason he was able to come back after assorted disappointments is the outlook he has on skating. It's important to him, but he knows it isn't everything. His advice to skaters who feel down is simple: "If they know in their heart that they love skating, then they should stick with it and try everything they can to make it work. If the time comes when they don't love it anymore, then they should set different goals for themselves. There are other things out there to do than skating." Although he considered hanging up his boots when things were going poorly for him, he knew in his heart that he had to continue.

Russian Ilia Kulik is one of the great jumpers to come out of the post-Lillehammer days. A World silver medalist in 1996, he trains in the United States, like so many skaters from the former Soviet Union. Many skaters from Europe and Asia, and some of the best Russian coaches, now make their home in America. Professionals spend most of their time in America because that's where most of their work is. Many top amateurs do so because it's getting harder to find good coaches and good ice back in their home countries.

One skater who always knows how to play the audience is France's Philippe Candeloro, World silver medalist in 1994, World bronze medalist in 1995, and Olympic bronze medalist in 1994 and 1998. Candeloro works hard to get into his characterizations. In his Olympic debut, he became the Godfather, in 1997 Napoleon, and in 1998 a

Russia's Ilia Kulik won the Olympic Men's gold medal in 1998.

Musketeer—not just skating to the music, but skating as the title characters, complete with mannerisms and attitude.

After Kristi Yamaguchi decided to focus solely on singles skating, Rudy Galindo experienced enough unfortunate circumstances to push less dedicated skaters over the edge. It was bad enough for him to lose the chance to repeat as National Champion in Pairs, which he had won with Yamaguchi in 1989 and 1990. But then, while attempting to make it as a singles skater, he lost his father, a brother, and two coaches.

Living in a mobile home out of economic necessity, he was determined to make his skating pay off. Coached for free by his sister Laura, he built up his singles technique. In 1996, at the age of twenty-six, he finally hit pay dirt. He gave a magical performance in his hometown of San Jose, one that left the audience in tears. Many considered it a fluke, but at the 1996 Worlds, he pulled off a bronze medal, then quickly turned pro. Perhaps more than any other skater, Galindo proved the power of patience and perseverance.

Post-Lillehammer Pairs and Ice Dancers

One of the most painful falls ever seen in the Winter Olympics was that of Germany's Mandy Wötzel and Ingo Steuer in Lillehammer, reminding all just how dangerous Pairs skating can be. The 1993 World silver medalists were poised to try for an Olympic medal when Wötzel's skate

One of the most popular skaters ever, France's Philippe Candeloro

Mandy Wötzel and Ingo Steuer have had their share of misfortunes on the ice.

blade got caught in an indentation in the ice, causing her to fall hard on her chin. Steuer almost fell on top of her, and ended up having to carry her off the ice in the middle of their long program.

Steuer has a few battle scars of his own, having suffered a cut lip from Wötzel's skate and a concussion from a lift mishap. But when they stay injury-free, they can be magnificent, as proven by the Worlds silver medal finish in 1996 and their gold medal finish in 1997.

Canadians Isabelle Brasseur and Lloyd Eisler were the most vocal in their opposition to the idea of pros reinstating as amateurs for the 1994 Winter Olympics. The team thrills audiences with their acrobatics, which helped them win Olympic bronze in 1992, behind the former Soviet teams of Mishkutenok and Dmitriev and Elena Bechke and Denis Petrov. They were perfectly situated to make a run for the Olympic gold in 1994. Though they ended up being the top amateur team, they were defeated in their goal by the two returning professional Russian teams of Gordeeva and Grinkov and Mishkutenok and Dmitriev.

Brasseur explains the team's feeling about professionals who reinstated: "We didn't understand why they would come back when they've already been there. We wouldn't go back because there are younger people who have trained for years, and for us to declare our eligibility for the Olympics in the last year means they wouldn't get to go. It may be their only chance to go to the Olympics."

Brasseur also has an opinion about the state of amateur Pairs skating: "I really believe a pair should be an overall look. They should have interaction between each other. They should have great lifts, a great death spiral, a great side-by-side spin, and an overall good package. I think more and more they're putting emphasis on the jumps, and they're lacking the Pairs package.

"A good Pairs package is Meno and Sand. You look at them and everything is good. Everything is smooth. Things are flowing. They were the only ones that didn't have a triple jump [in 1996], but they were the only ones that had a program that started from the

first seconds and flowed all the way through to the last seconds."

Jenni Meno and Todd Sand each won USFSA Nationals medals with different partners prior to 1993. After getting together just months earlier, they took the silver medal at Nationals in 1993 and won the next three titles, placing second in 1997 behind Kyoko Ina and Jason Dungien. In 1995 and 1996, they captured the bronze at Worlds. More important, they got married in 1995, although they claim that their artistry stems more from the blending of their styles than the fact that they're married.

Meno says: "We're so close and we spend so much time together that when we're out there [on the ice], we almost know what the other person is thinking. I think that helps us as a pair. It's nice to be out there competing with someone who loves you and someone whom you love."

Realizing how fortunate they are, Meno and Sand gave their grant money from the USFSA Athletes Support to the Junior Pairs Champions at the USFSA National Championships in order that the up-and-coming team could continue with their training.

The media loved Calla Urbanski and Rocky Marval, two Americans who had to work for a living to support their skating, Urbanski as a waitress and Marval as a truck driver. They took the U.S. silver medal in Pairs in 1991 and won the next two titles. But friction caused them to split up temporarily just before the 1994 Winter Olympics season.

Jenni Meno and Todd Sand found success and love with each other.

Calla Urbanski
and Rocky Marval,
nicknamed "the
waitress and the
truck driver."

Back together now, they enjoy their pro career, because the pressure is lifted off them and there are so many more opportunities to perform. And they're still referred to in the media as "the waitress and the truck driver." They say they did not create the image—CBS did. The network had a story to sell the public during the 1992 Winter Olympics, where they finished tenth. Urbanski was thirty-one at the time—the oldest skater on the ice by several years. She's proud to proclaim, "I paved the way, saying that 'You don't have to be eighteen to do it.'"

Marval is now married to Isabelle Brasseur.

The Russian/Ukrainian Ice Dancing team of Oksana Grishuk and Evgeny Platov hit the world scene with a bronze medal at the 1992 Worlds; in 1993, they moved up to silver. They then won the next four World titles and the 1994 and 1998 Winter Olympics. Their style is often one of frenetic activity and unabashed enthusiasm.

In the old days, they would bring in gas for their training rink's Zamboni; such were the difficulties they had to contend with as the former Soviet system reinvented itself. Perhaps that's one reason they enjoy living in America so much, along with so many other skaters from Russia. But they have one complaint about American television's treatment of Ice Dancing.

According to Oksana, who now goes by the single name of Pasha, "People enjoy watching Ice Dancing when we're on TV. But some competitions on TV cut out the dance parts. It makes us upset because we did our best job and got our best results. Most [people] don't have a chance to go and see performers in person, so they watch it on TV, and Ice Dancing gets cut off."

This is a phenomenon that indeed is true. Ice Dancing has traditionally been regarded as something less interesting for the public to watch. Americans, especially, like to be excited by figure skating. Perhaps Ice Dancing makes one think too much, as one has to concentrate on the beauty and flow in order to appreciate the sport. Watching singles skaters and Pairs is to witness sheer drama; they

Pasha (formerly Oksana Grishuk) and Evgeny Platov are the only couple to have won two Olympic gold medals in Ice Dancing.

pull off the aerial fireworks or they fall. For whatever reasons, Ice Dancing typically gets little coverage on American television.

To watch Ice Dancers is to experience romance. There rarely is any drama. In contrast to the microwaved fast food of singles skating and Pairs, Ice Dancing is a meal that takes time to heat up. But if one is patient, it can be the main course that is the most satisfying.

Nagano

Nagano Welcomes a Changed World

THE 1998 WINTER OLYMPICS IN NAGANO, JAPAN, were full of surprises: Tara Lipinski upset Michelle Kwan, and Lu Chen recovered remarkably from near oblivion. But the Winter Games also had their share of melancholy: Nicole Bobek plummeted, Todd Eldredge did not win a medal, and Elvis Stojko suffered a painful injury.

The spotlight focused upon renewed nationalism, which raised its head under the name "bloc judging."

Many geographic and political boundaries seemed to disappear, as several skaters from the former Soviet Union moved to the United States to enjoy substantially better training facilities. These included the Nagano Men's and Ice Dancing gold medalists—Ilia Kulik and Grishuk and Platov—coached by the versatile Tatiana Tarasova. Galina Zmievskaya (Petrenko's and Baiul's coach) also moved her home base. In addition to the incentive of better facilities in the United States, coaches from the former Soviet Union can make as much in two hours in the United States as they made in a month back home.

Four years before Nagano, the Boitano Rule had encouraged many professional skaters to reinstate and take another shot at Olympic glory. In 1998, not a single pro chose to take that step. Perhaps pros thought it would be too much work, or maybe they were concerned their standing in the public eye would be tarnished if they performed poorly. They may have recalled the subpar performances of so many of the reinstated pros in Lillehammer.

Ladies: America's 1-2 Punch

Despite pulling out of competitions and missing several crucial

weeks of practice because of a fractured bone in her foot, Michelle Kwan was stunning at the 1998 USFSA Nationals, earning fifteen Presentation 6.0s between her short and long programs. Up until then, no woman had received even a single 6.0 in a USFSA Nationals short program.

Naturally, Kwan became the favorite for Ladies' Olympic gold. A top skating journalist wrote that if Kwan were to fall in Nagano, her depth of artistry would still be enough to carry her through to the top of the medals podium.

Defending USFSA Nationals Champion Tara Lipinski hadn't fallen in a short program since 1996, but she did just that at the 1998 Nationals. She fought back from fourth place to capture the silver medal. Nicole Bobek finished with the bronze, seeming to have recovered from the 1997 loss of her coach at Worlds. Immediately, there was talk of an American 1-2-3 sweep of the Ladies' medals in Nagano.

The approaches of the American Ladies' Olympic Team members to the Winter Games were quite different. Kwan and Bobek took a safe approach, staying home to practice and arriving after the Olympics were well under way. Lipinski decided to experience the Olympics to the fullest—marching in the opening ceremonies, living in the Olympic village, and attending hockey games.

After the short program, Kwan and Lipinski sat 1-2, followed by Russia's Maria Butyrskaya, a self-proclaimed "romantic woman on the ice," in contrast to what she said was Lipinski's "childish skating." The two top Americans looked strong as they headed into the long program free skate.

The Ladies' free skate in Nagano is said to have been the greatest Ladies' event ever. Kwan skated superbly, but without the spark that ignited her soul at Nationals. She scored nine straight 5.9s in Presentation, but few counted on Lipinski's 5.8s and 5.9s in Presentation, earned by skating with boundless joy and charm. With

Michelle Kwan was the favorite leading into the 1998 Winter Olympics.

superior Technical Merit marks, Lipinski became the youngest Olympic Ladies' Champion in skating history, taking that honor away from Sonja Henie.

China's Lu Chen took bronze over Butyrskaya with an ethereal long program performance that was so delicate it seemed as if she was skating on a cloud. Her remarkable recovery came on the heels of a disastrous 1997, which saw her fail to qualify for the short program at Worlds.

Further down the ranking than one would expect, in tenth place, was potential medalist Surya Bonaly. Despite her placement, she created some of the loudest talk to come out of Nagano. She was still steaming over her short program Technical Merit scores of 4.9 to 5.7, an astounding range of judging inconsistency. She showed her contempt for the system by throwing in an illegal back flip near the end of her long program, then ended her show with her back to the judges.

And what about Bobek? She finished seventeenth in both the short and long programs, falling on several jumps, earning scores as low as 4.4. Every skater has bad days. But few have bad days that happen so publicly and at such an inopportune time. But at least she had a chance to compete. Germany's Tanja Szewczenko had been an Olympic medal favorite, as a result of winning some major international competitions. After courageously battling back from a serious foot injury and a life-threatening illness that had almost killed her, she caught the flu in Nagano and had to withdraw from the Olympics.

Tara Lipinski surprised many people, but not herself, in winning the 1998 Winter Olympics.

Lu Chen won a second Olympic bronze in 1998.

Men: Towering Triumphs and Devastating Defeats

Unlike the predicted Ladies' results, there was no clear leader heading into the Men's competition in Nagano. The only certainty was that there would be a new Men's Champion, as Alexei Urmanov had been forced out of competition earlier in the season with a groin injury.

Russian Ilia Kulik had pulled out of the European Championships with a pinched back nerve. But he was in no pain as he won the Olympic short program, then knocked off a quadruple toe loop as the first skater in the long program's final group. This set a standard that no other skater was able to match, making Kulik the first Men's skater to take the gold medal in his first Olympic appearance since Dick Button did so fifty years earlier.

Canada's Elvis Stojko, more than any other skater, can take credit for the technical revolution in Men's skating. He pulled off the first quadruple jump combined with any other jump, the first quad toe loop–double toe loop, and the first successful landing of a quad-triple combination. But he had long heard from the judges that he should be more artistic, more flowing, "softer" on the ice. He refused to pay attention to any of that, earning his three World Championships with his incredible technique, overshadowing the judges' reservations about his bombastic, martial arts–inspired style.

During the long program, many observers sensed that he was having trouble. He didn't even try his quad, even though Kulik had already landed one. He appeared slower than normal and lacked his typical spunk. At the end of his program, he grimaced in extreme pain and could barely make it off the ice, hardly seeming to notice his scores.

Only a handful of people knew that Stojko had injured a groin muscle a month before the Olympics. He didn't want any sympathy from the judges, choosing heroically to let his skating stand on its own merits. His coach, Doug Leigh, said that if there were a medal for courage, Stojko should get it.

Nagano was the fourth Olympics in a row that saw a Canadian enter competition as the reigning World Champion, each coached by Leigh. In every case, the Olympic gold medal proved out of reach, and Canada has yet to win its first Olympic Men's gold medal.

When the World Championships were in Japan in 1994, the Japanese audience fell head over heels in love with Philippe Candeloro and his antics. His popularity was still riding high when he returned for the Olympics, even though he finished no higher than ninth at the previous two Worlds. But the surprise bronze medalist from Lillehammer four years earlier proved he knows when to peak for maximum effect, capturing the bronze with a magnificently choreographed routine as a dashing Musketeer sword fighter. For sheer spectacle, it was one of the most splendid programs ever witnessed.

And with Candeloro's remarkable performance, former World Champion Todd Eldredge found himself in an uncomfortably familiar situation. Like Kurt Browning before him, he built up to an Olympic medal and didn't get one, even though he became the first skater since Dick Button to win five Men's USFSA titles. He added his fourth-place 1998 finish to his list of personally challenging Olympic experiences, having finished in tenth place in 1992 because of a back injury, and missing out on 1994 opportunities when he caught the flu prior to Nationals.

Entering the long program, he appeared tense, proceeding to water down a triple axel into a single, fumbling his triple-triple combination, and turning the second part of two combination jumps into double axels. He attempted to throw in a triple axel—and fell on it—at the end of his program, a gutsy move that had worked when he won the World Championship in 1996. Like Browning, he quite possibly left the Olympics with a giant "what if" hanging over him.

Because of his injury, Stojko didn't attempt a quad. Candeloro doesn't have one in his arsenal of jumps, and Eldredge (who attempted one and fell at Nationals) chose not to risk it in Nagano.

With Kulik performing one, the 1998 Winter Games became the first Olympics in which the quad determined the final results. Some think that the jump will be so common in the future that it will become a required element in Men's short programs.

Pairs: The Russians Still Have What It Takes

In Pairs competition in Nagano, Tamara Moskvina's teams, still coached in Russia, won gold and silver. This gave Russian skaters their tenth straight Olympic Pairs gold medal since 1964.

Oksana Kazakova and Artur Dmitriev came alive in the long program with a burning passion that was poetry on ice. Dmitriev became the first male Pairs skater to win Olympic gold twice with two different partners, first with Natalia Mishkutenok in 1992, and then with Kazakova.

Silver medalists Elena Bereznaia and Anton Sikharulidze had topped Kazakova and Dmitriev at the Champions Series finals and the European Championships. Since 1968, the winning Pair at every Europeans held in an Olympic year had gone on to win Olympic gold. But a fall by Sikharulidze in the short program dimmed their chances of winning, and both fell, with just seconds to go in the long program, as she was coming down from a star lift.

It might be said the real victory was in Bereznaia's even being on the ice. She had recovered from ongoing abuse from a previous partner and a serious injury that saw his blade slice open her skull during a side-by-side camel spin, the maneuver in which a leg of each skater is extended outward at head level while each rotates close to the other in unison. Soon after her recovery, she and Sikharulidze started to skate together, rapidly becoming a major international force.

Bronze medalists Mandy Wötzel and Ingo Steuer certainly had their share of accidents. Like Bereznaia, Wötzel also spent a few months in the hospital after being hit in the head with a previous partner's skate during a side-by-side camel spin. Then she experienced the horrible fall in the 1994 Olympics. Steuer endured a half dozen knee operations in addition to a cut lip and a concussion from lift mishaps. But it was an accident just two months prior to Nagano that almost kept them from going for a medal. Steuer's right arm was hit by the mirror of a car while he stood on the sidewalk in Germany, tearing shoulder ligaments and giving him lasting headaches and dizziness—two symptoms especially dangerous to someone responsible for safely lifting another skater over his head.

American Champions Kyoko Ina and Jason Dungjen made a valiant try for a medal, missing by just one spot. Their short program scores had them in first place from one judge and seventh from another, causing their coach to ask if the judges were all watching the same program. Others had wondered the same when Sikharulidze's fall in the short program didn't result in a mandatory deduction, and when Kazakova and Dmitriev won first place on the sheets of eight of the nine judges in the long program, but received fourth place on the sheet of the German judge. This led to concern that the German judge had tried to prop up the chances of his country's Wötzel and Steuer.

Jenni Meno and Todd Sand were forced to pull out of the 1998 USFSA Nationals when Meno bruised an ankle bone just hours before the long program. The USFSA sent them to the Olympics, though, after considering their past performance results. Meno spent a few weeks off the ice for rehabilitation before Nagano, but falls reduced them to finishing in eighth place overall.

Dance: "Bloc Judging" Exposed

Twenty-two years after Ice Dancing was first allowed in the Winter Olympics, some people still wondered whether it should be an Olympic sport. The people asking these questions were not comforted by claims in Nagano that Ice Dancing results are sometimes fixed.

To many, Pasha (Oksana Grishuk) and Evgeny Platov seemed the predetermined Olympic Ice Dancing winners. They came into

Russia's Anjelika
Krylova and Oleg
Ovsiannikov are
perfect examples
of classical Russian
Ice Dancing
emotion and drama.

Nagano with a twenty-one-event winning streak stretching all the way back to the 1994 Winter Olympics, and they weren't penalized for falls in three different competitions leading up to the Olympics. (Falls in Ice Dancing are practically unheard of.) And although Pasha almost fell during the first compulsory dance of the Olympics, the team was placed first by seven of the nine judges.

However, in the free dance, the team delivered one of the most remarkable and captivating programs seen since Torvill and Dean's *Bolero. Memorial Requiem* exuded a quality that made viewers afraid to breathe, lest they miss something. And when it was all over, Pasha and Platov became the first Ice Dancers to repeat as Olympic gold medalists.

Russians Anjelika Krylova and Oleg Ovsiannikov took the silver medal, and the French team of Marina Anissina (a former Russian skater) and Gwendal Peizerat took the bronze with a thoroughly captivating role-playing program to *Romeo and Juliet*.

The cries of bloc judging were loudest from the camp of Canada's fourth-place Shae-Lynn Bourne and Victor Kraatz, bronze medalists at the 1996 and 1997 World Championships. Despite skating clean compulsory dances, they were already out of the gold medal hunt by the end of the first compulsory dance, in which they finished fifth. This led their coach, Natalia Dubova, to issue the charge of bloc judging among some of the judges.

Bloc judging is where a number of judges from different countries get together and agree to help one anothers' skaters by voting in a predetermined manner. A pair would practically have

Shae-Lynn Bourne and Victor Kraatz are shown "etching a deep line."

to break their legs on the ice to change the results. Dubova's charges were largely based on the fact that the same five judges placed certain teams in the exact same high positions for the compulsories, while all the other judges rated the same teams lower, and the five judges placed other teams in low positions when all the other judges had the same teams in higher positions.

Bloc judging or not, the results in Nagano were very predictable. The only change in position among the top twenty-four couples caused by the free dance results was an exchange of positions between teams in twentieth and twenty-first place. Once couples got set up in the compulsories, they tended to stay put. This led the president of the ISU to say he would ask the federation's congress to increase the value of the free dance, which would decrease the value of the compulsory phase and supposedly hinder bloc judging. Only in Ice Dancing is the final phase not worth more than what comes before it.

Other news in Ice Dancing was that, for the first time ever, vocals were allowed for the original dance, the second phase of the competition. It was shocking for some to hear Elvis Presley and other singers scream out during the required jive rhythm, seeming to blur the lines of distinction between competition and exhibition programs.

Once again, Ice Dancing appeared to be pulled in opposite directions. The leading practitioners of pure Ice Dancing (as defined by the rule book) were Bourne and Kraatz, whose *Riverdance* brought a massive amount of footwork to the rink. The most obvious proponents of Ice Dancing as Ice Theater were Pasha and Platov, leading the discipline into new, uncharted territory.

The old question from the 1980s remained: Is it ballroom dancing on ice—or can it, and should it, be something more?

part **Four**

Fashions

A S SOON AS A SKATER GLIDES ONTO THE ICE FOR A performance, her choice of costuming creates expectations in the minds of judges and fans. Realizing this, the top Ladies' skaters in the world sometimes spend thousands of dollars on custom-made costumes, to give themselves that added push over their competition. For her 1994 Winter Olympics program, Nancy Kerrigan commissioned an original outfit from Vera Wang, one of the best-known designers of wedding gowns for wealthy people. Such taste does not come cheap.

Men's costumes are quite a bit simpler and less expensive. Sometimes sequins will be splashed on for effect, but typically the costumes are not too extravagant. Whatever the gender, the outfit must fit perfectly, allowing for freedom of movement, and must enhance the skater rather than be the main attraction. Costumes won't make a skater, but a bad costume, or one that is too gaudy, could distract the judges enough that it could break the skater. The goal of a custom costume designer, then, is to get a distinctive look while not going overboard.

Deborah Nelson, president of Satin Stitches, has made costumes for countless skaters for more than a quarter century. As a costume designer and creator, she is always searching for new, durable fabrics that will move with the skater's body.

Nelson finds it necessary to stay current with the latest design trends off the ice, drawing inspiration from designs for high fashion, activewear, ballroom dance, pageant gowns, and Broadway and film costuming. Of today's costumes, she says: "Instead of the heavily beaded dresses of past years, emphasis is on pure styling with

Skating costumes made by Satin Stitches

distinguished accents. Judicious use of rhinestones and beaded and sequined appliqués gives the hint of glitz that a costume needs to add sparkle to a performance."

Careful attention is given to costumes for Men's skaters so that the look is masculine. Shirts are designed as full body suits so that they always appear to be perfectly tucked in.

The total look of the costume goes beyond the blouse and skirt or pants and shirt. Sometimes it even goes as far as incorporating matching boot covers. Not all skaters can afford to buy a special set of boots in a color matching the costume, so boot covers are a good way to get around that.

On the other end of the wardrobe spectrum are the touring ice shows. Competitive skaters for the most part have to take care of their own costumes. (One popular story is told of Brian Boitano's dying his tights in a hotel sink and hanging them out the window to dry.) But big touring companies often travel with a person whose job it is to keep all the costumes in top shape between performances and to fix problems when they occur during performances.

Wardrobe master Roger Bathurst has spent a number of seasons with *Champions on Ice*. He always has safety pins available for last-second emergency repairs, and while he worked with *Holiday on Ice*, he even sewed performers into their costumes when a zipper broke at the last moment.

Bathurst has taken care of beaded costumes that cost several thousand dollars. The skaters are performing in exhibition, so, unlike the trend toward simplicity that Deborah Nelson sees in competitive skating, Bathurst sees the skaters go to the opposite extreme, toward glamour and glitz. The top Ladies' skaters use a lot of chiffon and Lycra. The Men's skaters lean toward gabardine, a material that always looks nice and pressed and keeps its crease. But while the Ladies' skaters of the *Champions on Ice* tour attempt to create a major ice show look with a lot of sequins and beads, the Men's skaters are increasingly skating in T-shirt–type tops and slacks, with some of the shirts bought right off the rack.

Blades

Blades don't get much press in the skating journals and are not often spoken of as separate items apart from skating boots. When people speak of "skates," they are usually talking about the combination of the blade and the boot.

No one today thinks much about E. V. Bushnell's 1850 creation of a skate boot that, for the first time, contained a screw-on steel blade. But because of his invention, the thin pieces of metal making up the blade allow skaters to glide across the surface of the ice at great

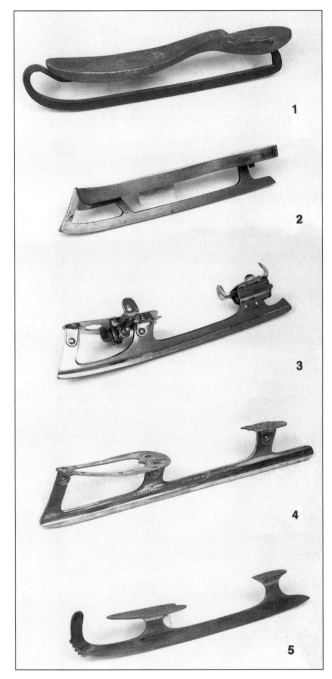

The evolution of skating blades is seen
in this series of photos.

speed. With screw-on blades, they can jump and rotate without fear of the blades separating upon landing. It seems remarkable that everything skaters do, they do on a piece of metal just over one-eighth of an inch wide.

Because sharpening blades requires a grinding wheel and an expert and steady hand, few skaters sharpen their own. If the blades aren't sharpened properly, skaters will have a difficult time attaining the speeds necessary for jumping. There can be no nicks or burrs in the metal; these would slow one down or even trip one up.

A careful sharpening will leave a smooth but sharp inside edge and outside edge on the bottom of each blade, with an equally smooth hollow and rounded concave groove between the two edges. (The inside edge is the edge closest to the other skate. The outside edge is farthest from the other skate.) These edges prevent skaters from sliding to the side and allow them to grip the ice in order to push off for propulsion. The gripping of the ice also allows them to glide, jump, and steer themselves in straight lines or curves. Skaters typically favor one or the other edge unless traveling in a straight line.

And as the area between the edges is concave and not flat, so are the blades not flat from front to back. There is a slight, almost imperceptible curve to the blade, allowing for a smaller part of the blade to come into contact with the ice at any one time. This makes it easier for the skater to maneuver and skate in curved forms.

Figure skate blades are noticeably different from hockey and speed skate blades in that they have teeth, notches in the metal in the front part of the blade, which assist in the takeoffs of jumps and spins. Most skaters who have achieved any level of proficiency will find themselves skating on one of two blade brands: John Wilson or Mitchell & King (better known as MK). Both brands are made in the same factory in England, the two companies having merged in 1997.

Serious skaters skate on blades that have a tempered steel chromium finish, as opposed to the cheaper nickel plating found on some less expensive blades. Incidentally, Ice Dancing blades are shorter than Pairs and singles blades. This allows the couple to do fancy footwork close to each other's blades without the blades' coming in contact.

Boots

While the choice in brands for top blades is quite limited, there is a larger variety of brands and styles of boots available for all levels of skaters. The most important thing a skater needs to remember when choosing a boot is fit, fit, and fit. Without a proper fit, the boot just won't work well and the skater might experience all sorts of problems, from blisters and calluses to ankle injuries.

A serious, growing skater generally wants to have a half size of room to grow into, with a little space left at the end of the big toe. Some parents think it's okay to save money by having their developing skater wear an extra pair of socks to fill in a pair of skates that is way too large. This is a bad idea. Boots that are too wide will

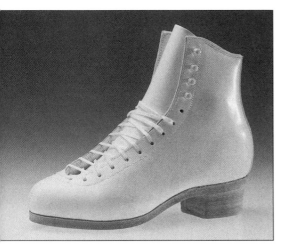

An SP-Teri boot

crease and break down. In the other direction, boots that are too narrow—used after a skater should have moved to a larger size—will cause cramps.

Department store boots often come in just one width and are usually available only in full sizes. A good-quality boot line will be available in several widths and half sizes, such as the line of boots by SP-Teri.

Besides the additional widths and sizes, other factors separate a typical department store skating boot from one of quality. A skater should look for good, firm leather in the ankle area. Soles and heels should be made of leather instead of rubber. Better boots have ankle padding and will have foam padding (instead of less expensive felt padding) on the tongue.

Some mass-merchandised boots combine the soles and heels into one unit, which is not recommended. Also, the blades are sometimes riveted on, so one cannot adjust them. A better boot will allow for the blades to be screwed on, making them adjustable in the future.

To be properly fitted to boots, a skater will go to a local skate shop (which is often located at a training rink). The shop personnel will then put the skater's feet on a measuring device that will determine the foot size for a single specific manufacturer. (Each manufacturer has its own measuring scale.) The skater is measured for length, and then the ball of the foot is measured to determine width. Only then will appropriate boots be tried on. The boot is fitted to the foot; then the blade is fitted to the boot. Skaters with hand-me-down blades should avoid the temptation to go with a boot just because the blade fits.

A boot that is too big will feel comfortable when new. But when the skater skates on it, many problems may occur. The skater may experience blisters and heel slippage. She won't properly feel her toe picks or the edges of the blades. And, she will often re-lace the boot in a futile attempt to get a tighter fit.

One should never discount the importance of a skater's boots' feeling just right. In 1984, at the Sarajevo, Yugoslavia, Winter Olympics, Barbara Underhill and Paul Martini were considered favorites to win the gold medal in Pairs. Underhill felt very uncomfortable in her new boots, which contributed to a fall in the short program—destroying their chances for a medal—and caused her to single a side-by-side double jump in the long program. The team finished in seventh place.

After the Olympics, Underhill, at the suggestion of fellow Canadian skater Brian Orser, took her new blades off her new boots and put them on a pair of old, comfortable boots. With everything feeling right and proper, the team stunned the skating community by winning the World Championship a few weeks later. Underhill attributed the difference in performance to being comfortable in her boots, a vivid lesson for all skaters.

How Ice Is Made

Many venues where touring ice companies perform are arenas that host hockey games, and as such, the buildings already contain ice-making equipment. But sometimes a tour will visit a venue where ice-making equipment is not available. How does the ice get made? The company brings in its own.

No, touring companies don't travel with ice, but they do travel with the equipment necessary to make it. This is where someone like Donald Yontz of Entertainment Production Services comes in. Yontz has been around skating since 1968 and once was a principal skater in *Ice Capades*. He has been at the forefront of ice making for traveling ice shows and has developed some specialized equipment for his state-of-the-art ice-making process.

At the heart of Yontz's system is a five-and-a-half-inch-deep frame not unlike that of a water bed. A plastic liner holds in the water. An inch of high-density foam insulation is laid on the floor over the liner, over which the refrigeration coils are set. Then the rink is flooded and water fills up the area inside the plastic liner. Rinks can be adjusted to fit just about any size stage.

The coils under the ice are an adaptation of solar collector panels like the type one finds throughout Yontz's home state of Florida. They are set in mats known in the ice industry as Yontz Mats. Each mat consists of five three-eighths-inch tubes that are in essence rubber pipes, connected to as many other Yontz Mats as needed. Refrigeration fluid moves through these pipes, bringing in cold to freeze the ice and keep it frozen, and more important, removing heat in the process. Only sixty-five gallons per minute of brine solution— the refrigeration fluid—move through the floor, which isn't a lot, considering that the amount is spread across the entire floor. Quite a bit of heat is moved away from the ice with a very small amount of fluid.

The brine solution is pumped into a machine that sits on a truck outside the venue, a machine very similar to the ones used for stationary ice rinks. A big engine with cooling fans absorbs the heat from the warmed brine; then Glycol, acting like an antifreeze, cools the brine by extracting the heat before the compressor pump sends the brine back through the Yontz Mats for another pass.

Once the ice is set, the crew turns off the cooling machine and lets the ice melt. When it is refrozen, it forms a much more solid surface than before and is considered "cured." This process also helps eliminate air pockets formed during the initial freezing, which could be a problem if a skater were to land on one and crash through the ice.

It takes twenty-four hours to put in a rink completely, from carrying everything needed into the venue to laying it down, setting it up, filling it up, and letting it cure. Only about three of those hours are spent laying down the floor.

One big problem in keeping the ice at the right temperature is the heat produced by the lights used on the stage. When the lights are too hot, the compressor has to work overtime, which risks making the ice too hard. The harder the ice is, the sharper a skater's blades need to be, and the ice tends to shatter when skaters come down from jumps. Keeping ice at the right temperature is a delicate and vitally important process.

Because traveling with a Zamboni is not viable for small rinks, the ice is resurfaced by filling the bad ruts with slush, scraping off the snow, and spreading water over the surface and letting it harden. This has to be accomplished in a short time during intermissions, and the ice may not be totally frozen when skaters first get back on the surface.

Once the performance is over, workers walk onto the ice with twenty-pound poles that have sledgehammers attached to the bottom. They pound the ice and break it up, dumping the pieces outside. To thaw the ice on the stage by heating the coils (and then siphoning off the water) would take a prohibitive amount of time.

Because skating tours will often need portable ice rinks in tour stops just a day apart, Yontz has multiple crews and sets of equipment. He has even produced ice surfaces for outdoor venues in warm locations, such as Las Vegas, Nevada, and at Sea World in San Diego, California.

Z Is for Zamboni

Let's face it: The one star on the ice that everyone loves does not stand upright on two blades. The one star on the ice that is popular from one generation to the next has never been entered in competition, has never won a medal, and has never turned pro. And yet, this star has been seen in practically every ice rink around the world.

Everyone loves the Zamboni Ice Resurfacer. Every skater would love to be adored as much as the public adores the Zamboni. Who among us wouldn't jump at the chance to drive a Zamboni around the rink, preparing the ice surface for the next round of eager skaters? After all, even the best skaters have an occasionally bad performance and don't receive the applause they would hope for after they're done. But the Zamboni . . . well, the Zamboni *always* receives applause when it completes its task.

A miniature Zamboni is even used by Snoopy and Woodstock and their gang of bird friends from the "Peanuts" comic strip, resurfacing the ice of a birdbath in between periods of the troupe's hockey games.

Make no mistake: A Zamboni isn't a glamorous vehicle. It has a top speed of only ten miles per hour. The most popular model weighs 6,580 pounds when empty and 8,780 pounds when full of water. However, glamorous or not, the machines have the distinction of having been featured on their own commemorative ice hockey trading card, right along with all top hockey players in the National Hockey League.

Why the need for Zambonis? Since the time of the first artificially produced ice surfaces in the mid- to late 1800s, ice rink caretakers have attempted to create consistently perfect ice surfaces. "Perfect" ice had to be the right temperature and the right consistency—not too mushy and not too hard. It also had to be smooth and stay smooth. Making ice of the right temperature and consistency was the easy part. The hard part was keeping it smooth after numerous blades cut into the ice, marring the surface and creating etchings in the ice that could catch the skates of later skaters and cause them to fall.

Even when an ice surface is sitting with no skaters, dust and dirt in the air settle on it and have to be removed. Ice rink caretakers always had to make sure their ice surface was not only smooth but also clean. The surface also had to be flat, and a specified ice thickness had to be maintained. And all this sometimes had to be done rather quickly, by hand.

In the days before the Zamboni, resurfacing the ice was a com-

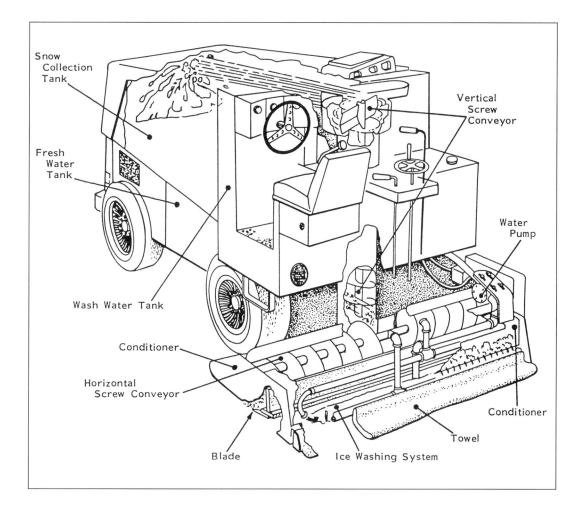

Snow Collection Tank

Fresh Water Tank

Vertical Screw Conveyor

Water Pump

Wash Water Tank

Conditioner

Horizontal Screw Conveyor

Conditioner

Towel

Blade

Ice Washing System

THE INNER WORKINGS OF A ZAMBONI ICE RESURFACER

1. The ice surface is first shaved by the blade.
2. The ice scrapings are picked up by the augerlike horizontal screw conveyor, which transfers the scrapings to the center.
3. The vertical screw conveyor lifts the scrapings to the top and throws them into the snow collection tank.
4. The ice washing system cleans the ice surface, and the water pump sucks up the dirty water into the wash water tank.
5. The towel component of the conditioner spreads the clean water in a thin, even layer.
6. The snow collection tank is emptied after the Zamboni leaves the rink surface. Every several resurfacings, the water in the wash water tank is replaced with clean water.

plex procedure. A group of three to five workers had to scrape down the ice surface with giant hand-pushed scrapers and then get the shavings to the end of the rink for disposal. For a better surface, the rink would occasionally be shaved by a planer towed behind a tractor. After the rink was planed down, the ice surface was washed off with a hose to eliminate dirt. The workers then had to use giant hand-pushed rubber squeegees to push off the dirty water and to smooth the water evenly across the surface so it would form level ice. Then a very thin film of fresh, clean water was flooded over the rink so that the top surface of the ice would cover up any ripples and offer the skaters the best possible skating surface. Needless to say, the act of resurfacing ice was very time-consuming, taking up to two hours.

In 1940, Frank J. Zamboni started down the road to making history. He opened up a rink in Paramount, California, and became increasingly frustrated with the time and labor needed to resurface the ice. Three years later, he began to experiment with a variety of mechanical methods of resurfacing the ice, starting out with a sled towed behind a tractor. The results were less than impressive.

By 1949, Zamboni had developed the Model A Zamboni Ice Resurfacer, a single machine able to pick up a sufficient amount of old ice, spread water across the entire surface, and smooth it out to a glossy sheen, all in one pass.

Essentially, this is how the Zamboni Ice Resurfacer works: A sharp blade shaves the ice down to a depth that is controlled by the operator. The old ice is moved to the center of the blade, where a rotating screw encased in a tube lifts the old ice up and transfers it to a holding tank, where it will stay until disposed of. Clean water is washed across the ice surface, flushing out the dirt left in the exposed grooves of ice. The water, now dirty, is vacuumed up by a pump, passed through a filter, and returned into the water tank. A thin layer of fresh, hot water is spread evenly onto the ice from the very back of the machine. The hot water soaks into the ice, creating a strong bond and a glassy, smooth surface. (The introduction of the hot water onto the frozen ice is why it looks like steam is rising from the surface after the Zamboni passes by.)

No one knows how long it would have taken Frank Zamboni's machine to become world famous if it were not for one little fortunate coincidence. In 1950, Sonja Henie and the cast of her new show, the *Sonja Henie Ice Review*, ended up practicing at Zamboni's Paramount rink. Henie saw the value of the machine and asked Zamboni to build a second one. She took it on tour through the United States, Canada, and Europe, introducing much of the world to the invention. When managers of other ice rinks saw the Zamboni do in minutes—and better—what it took a number of workers hours to do, orders started to arrive in Paramount for more machines. *Ice Capades* soon started to travel with one and gave the machine further exposure.

The Zambonis of today are sleek and stylish compared with the early machines. There is a variety of different models—some are huge, and one very small model is towed behind a garden tractor. Some Zambonis are even made to suck the water off of artificial turf stadium surfaces. There have been more than six thousand shipped in the half century since the first Zamboni Ice Resurfacer was made, and they are now seen throughout the world in about sixty countries. But the machine's main purpose remains as it always has been—to resurface ice surfaces quickly for the benefit of skaters everywhere.

Today's Zambonis are sleek and stylish.

Coaches

THE ONLY TIME THE PUBLIC IS AWARE OF COACHES is when they are seen on televised amateur competitions, sitting next to their students in the "kiss and cry" area as they wait for and finally witness the judges' scores. The coach then often gives the skater either an enthusiastic or sympathetic embrace.

A figure skater not quite competitive on the national level might be able to get by without a lot of support staff. If he is extremely creative himself, he might be able to do his own choreography. He might get by without a costume designer. He might not need an athletic trainer, even though, for his health, one would be recommended. Perhaps he could do without a dance instructor.

But no skater can do without a coach.

Coaches are the unsung heroes of skating. They guide and direct skaters through the first steps on the ice, the first spins, the first jumps, the first competitions, the first successes, and the first failures. Coaches make sure skaters are learning proper technique. Sometimes a skater will think he knows how to do something, and to his way of thinking, how he's doing it is good enough. But coaches look beyond what the skater sees, studying the technique to find and correct basic flaws.

If a skater is learning something not quite right, it may look just fine to most people, but to his coach all sorts of warning signs go up. The coach knows that, without corrections as soon as possible, the skater might be hindered in the future. It's always easier to correct problems in the early stages, before the skater has to unlearn physical muscle memory and mental approaches to executing a specific element.

Coach Frank Carroll shows Michelle Kwan how a proper layback form should feel and look.

The coach, therefore, strives to push the skater as far as possible. Coaches are not paid to be loved. Skaters don't always want to go through the program one more time, or practice a specific jump over and over until they can do it in their sleep, or eat right and get enough rest. Or they might fight the idea of spending time with a choreographer or changing their diet. But with a firm coach directing them and telling them what they *need* to hear and not necessarily what they *want* to hear, they will do what's needed to succeed.

Why is Brian Boitano still coached by Linda Leaver (his only coach since he started skating in group lessons in 1972) whenever he's home? His answer is "Feedback. Something may feel right, but it doesn't look right. Every skater needs someone who knows their skating well enough to say, 'You know, it just doesn't *look* right. The landings are weird, the height isn't good.'"

A good coach knows a skater better than the skater knows himself.

Choreographers

Good coaches also know when they alone cannot take a skater to the next level. The best case in point was after Boitano's 1987 Worlds silver medal finish. Leaver contacted the famous choreographer Sandra Bezic and brought her and Boitano together to work on his style and musical interpretation. In 1987, some felt that Boitano was more interested in nailing a quad jump at Worlds than he was in delivering an artistically balanced program that made an emotional connection with judges and fans.

Bezic has a reputation for reaching into a skater's soul and helping him become one with the music, getting him to put himself into the music, and making him hear the music in a different way from what he thought possible. The progress she made with Boitano in one season was stunning, and as a consequence his 1988 Olympic gold medal performance ranks as one of the most magnificently emotional and creative programs ever delivered on an international stage.

Eight years later, another choreographer accomplished stunning results with a top-level skater. Lori Nichol started working with Michelle Kwan, a student of famed coach Frank Carroll, three years before her 1996 Worlds victory over defending World Champion Lu Chen. She tried to get Michelle to "be herself," to express her inner self rather than imitate others—in other words, to be creative.

When it came time to work on the sophisticated *Salome's Dance* long program of 1996, Nichol played a part of the music and asked Kwan, "Well, what would you do to this music?" Kwan replied, "Well, Brian [Boitano] would do this," proceeding to show Nichol all the things Brian might do with the same music. Then she showed Nichol what Oksana Baiul might do.

Nichol looked at her and asked, "Well, if someone were going to imitate *you*, what would they do?" Kwan thought about that and said, "Well, that's an interesting question." They talked about who *she* was as an artist, exploring how she could find the artist within her. Kwan was learning how to "skate from the heart."

Kwan remembers the experience. "At the beginning I was thinking, What are you talking about? I always wanted to skate like Brian and Oksana, and I finally found out that everyone's original and everyone has their own style. I had to find it from within and not just rely on Lori giving me the movements."

Prior to the experience that changed Kwan's perspective, she simply took the choreographic movements Nichol gave her and did them with no

Choreographer Lori Nichol accomplished stunning results with student Michelle Kwan.

argument. Says Nichol, "I know it sounds strange, but I want the arguments. I want to hear 'I don't like that, I like this,' because then the movements are also coming from her. She's moving how *she* wants to move."

When done right, the process of choreography is one of give-and-take between skater and choreographer. The choreographer may conceive a movement and then show it to the skater, who in turn tries it out and offers another spin on it. They each inspire the other to come up with different ways of interpreting the music.

After a show is put together, a skater may not see the choreographer for quite some time, as he primarily works with his coach during that period to polish the techniques needed to execute the program flawlessly. The skater may run into the choreographer now and then to polish the creative part of the program, to keep it fresh and lively. Coaches and choreographers try hard to work hand in hand, frequently discussing movements with each other. And in Kwan's case, they had her work with a Russian ballet teacher to learn how to convey facial expressions.

In some ways, a choreographer is like an architect who designs a building, while a coach is like a structural engineer who figures out how to build it.

Athletic Trainers

Through the training process, skaters have to take care of their bodies. Their coaches may have them consult with a dietitian to make sure they're eating right, a doctor to make sure they're healthy inside and out, and an athletic trainer to keep them limber and free of pain.

Eric Lang is one of the best-known athletic trainers in the business. Although he works at the Center for Sports Medicine in San Francisco, California, he spends much of the year traveling with *Champions on Ice* and also provides his services at some professional competitions.

Lang discusses some of the problems faced by figure skaters: "Skaters generally experience a lot of lower back problems due to compression from jumps putting a lot of load on the spine. On a blade that's so narrow, there's less area to spread out the compression forces, so more load goes up the spine, causing many lower back problems.

"Skaters on tour for several months—who are on planes and buses more than they're on the ice—experience a lot of problems. Muscles get tight and shortened from being in the sitting position all day, and that can have mechanical consequences for the back. The life of being on tour is more problematic and produces more back injuries than the actual skating."

But preventive maintenance is always preferable to having to fix skaters after they're "broken." Lang teaches skaters "about posture, how to sit, and how to do stretching exercises to stabilize their lower back while they're sitting. I show them how to carry their luggage and other things that seem mundane to most people. Athletes in such great condition don't tend to think about everyday body mechanics."

Lang points out, "It's said that eighty percent of the people in the world are going to have back pain sometime in their lives. Skaters are even more at risk because of all the sitting they do [traveling to performances], and then they go from being totally sedentary to doing explosive, ballistic activity on the ice where the compression forces are so great."

And for the young skaters out there who wonder what sort of advice Lang might give them: "They should do hip flexor flexibility and upper trunk/torso–arm strength exercises to help rotations and jumps. They should work with weights for basic strength and not forget to do lots of stretching."

Managers: Don't Leave Home without One

Skating is more than an art form and an athletic endeavor—it's a business. With all the opportunities open to skaters today, they need someone to help them take care of their business interests so they can concentrate on keeping their skating in top form.

Every top-level skater needs a manager to pull everything together. The manager sometimes is also her agent, and sometimes the manager coordinates other agents on the skater's behalf. There is a difference between a sports manager and an agent, but it's a distinction that is often lost. While the manager coordinates agents and oversees a skater's overall career, agents tend to be specialists in a particular field, such as commercials, book deals, and competitions or exhibitions. Sometimes a single person, a manager/agent, will do it all. For the sake of this explanation, let's assume that the word *manager* also means manager/agent.

Michael Rosenberg, president of Marco Entertainment, is one of the best-known managers in the business. His clients have included numerous Olympic and World Champions and other skaters who are less well known. Marco Entertainment and IMG (International Management Group) are the two best-known management companies for figure skaters.

Rosenberg points out that a star figure skater's basic earning potential goes far beyond the competitive ice rink. The skater will also have many opportunities to earn income from tours, TV shows, specials, commercials, books, and other merchandise. Once she becomes famous, she needs someone to intervene for her, field calls from interested parties, initiate calls to possible interested parties, and establish contacts between those parties and the skater.

Someone like Rosenberg will negotiate the contract and work out details such as how much the skater is going to get paid for her services. A manager also arranges for travel and lodging, makes sure the skater will have a proper dressing room, and finds out where the skater will be in the show order and even in the final bow. Afterward, the manager collects the money being paid to the skater and forwards it to the skater's account.

Periodically, the manager discusses with the skater inquiries that

Manager/agent Michael Rosenberg with client Rudy Galindo

were received and helps her decide which opportunities are in her best interest. It is important to remember that the manager does not make decisions for the skater. The skater is always in charge of what she will and won't do. The manager just points out the pluses and minuses of each opportunity and makes recommendations when asked.

In short, the skater concerns herself with working with the people who can help her be successful on the ice—her coach, choreographer, costume designer, athletic trainer, and dance instructor. The skater is in charge of concentrating on her technique, musical numbers, total look, and technical proficiency. The manager concerns himself with everything else.

Skating Explodes on TV
Since the 1994 Winter Olympics in Lillehammer, Norway, the media have become extremely interested in figure skating. It seems hardly

a week goes by without a skating special on television. During the late fall, winter, and early spring months, one might find oneself having to choose which skating events to watch live and which to tape for later viewing. It wasn't always this way.

According to Michael Rosenberg of Marco Entertainment, skating has always been a popular sport: It combines glamour, sport, and art into one package. It is appealing because of its beauty, strength, suspense, speed, and drama. But it was not a sport that garnered overwhelming interest from the public.

In 1988, the Calgary, Alberta, Winter Olympics offered the public two highly publicized matchups, dubbed by the media the Battle of the Brians (Boitano versus Orser, both doing military programs) and Duel of the Carmens (Katarina Witt versus Debi Thomas, both doing music from the Georges Bizet opera). The public took an interest in the matchups. How could it not? Listening to the media hype, one could be forgiven for mistaking the two impending head-to-head matchups for upcoming professional wrestling bouts.

And in the hype, one simple fact was lost: Skaters don't skate "against" one another. They go out, do their best, and are supposed to be judged by how well or poorly they do, not by how well or poorly someone else skates.

But the public ate up the hype, and for the first time ever figure skating got the highest ratings of any Olympic sport on American television. Figure skating tours and shows started selling out their seating capacity, doing big, big business. The television networks saw that skating was great drama, perfect for TV.

In 1991, American Kristi Yamaguchi won the World Championship, making her the leading contender for the 1992 Winter Olympic crown in Albertville, France. This heightened interest among American viewers, and after she became the first American woman to win the Olympic Ladies' Championship since Dorothy Hamill in 1976, interest in skating tours and skating on TV was further stimulated. Suddenly there were five skating tours crossing the continent instead of two, and more hours of prime time skating could be seen on TV.

In 1994, the dam burst.

First was the clubbing of Nancy Kerrigan's knee at a practice session at the 1994 USFSA Championships, followed by the suspicions that teammate Tonya Harding was somehow involved, the eventual confirmation of those suspicions, and Harding's legal fight to stay on the U.S. Olympic Team. This was better than the most tawdry soap opera. The network evening news followed the story breathlessly as the Olympics approached, and the world watched not only the noose starting to close around Harding but also Kerrigan's rapid recuperation, painful physical rehabilitation, and her triumphant return to training on the ice.

By the time the Olympics began, a few weeks after the clubbing incident, the world was worked up by the suspense and impending on-ice matchup of Harding and Kerrigan. The public knew what restaurants Harding was eating in and what stores Kerrigan was shopping in. They became two of the most watched people on the planet.

Finally, after all the ballyhoo, the night arrived of the Ladies' short programs. TV viewership went through the roof, placing fourth among all American television broadcasts ever. The Ladies' long program was the sixth highest-rated TV broadcast in history, with an estimated one billion people watching worldwide.

Since 1994, televised skating events are said to grab higher ratings than many other big sporting events—higher than the Masters in golf, Wimbledon in tennis, the All-Star Game and World Series in baseball, the National Hockey League All-Star Game, and the National Basketball Association Finals. Figure skating has become the second most popular spectator sport in the United States, behind football.

American interest was high for the 1998 Winter Olympics,

because two Americans—Michelle Kwan and Tara Lipinski, each with a World Championship title to her name—were going for the Ladies' gold. And an American former World Champion—Todd Eldredge—and Canadian World Champion Elvis Stojko were going for the Men's gold. Four of the biggest names in amateur skating, and all were from North America.

But some of the suspense was missing from the Nagano, Japan, festivities. Because of the time zone differences between the United States and Japan, the televised events were broadcast on a tape-delayed basis. Hours before the skating broadcasts, results had been posted on the Internet and announced on radio and TV. Ratings suffered tremendously.

In the long run, however, the TV ratings from the 2002 Winter Olympics in Salt Lake City, Utah, have the potential to be stronger than those from the Lillehammer games. Because of the location—within the United States—the competitions will be shown live, not tape-delayed. Advertisers can expect to pay top dollar to have their names and products tied in to the events.

Media Frenzy

Canadian Gia Guddat has made quite a name for herself as a professional, as a designer of skating clothes, and as a skating teacher. She has also been one of the biggest hits, with sometime partner Gary Beacom, on the extensive tour now known as *Champions on Ice*. She has perfected the art of skating on four skates (two on the feet and two on the hands) at once, an innovation one has to see in person even to begin to comprehend.

Like all skaters, she has witnessed the media frenzy and sometimes the overenthusiasm of some fans. But her perspective is different. Because she was never on TV as an amateur and doesn't compete in televised professional contests, she can walk through a crowd of cameras or fans and not be noticed. This gives her a chance to observe without being observed.

According to Guddat, the media image of a skater is now more important than the skating itself. Nicole Bobek was a victim of media image making, portrayed for some time as a "wild girl out of control." Those who knew Bobek realized that wasn't true, but in the time after the Harding/Kerrigan incident, someone needed to fill in the media vacuum. Says Guddat, "[Bobek] just can't go out and skate anymore. It's a full-time job for her to try to project the right, more accurate image of what she's really like. She has to be careful of how she dresses, how she acts, and what she says. All the skaters are starting to face that. I think the skaters have a more difficult role now in that what they do on the ice may not be the major story once the media gets hold of it."

Indeed, it seems that we are beginning to know almost too much about the thoughts and deeds of our favorite skaters. Guddat feels that "the media blitz over the Tonya/Nancy affair gave people too much access to skaters' personal lives, which opened the door to people wanting to know everything about skaters behind-the-scenes."

Perhaps there has never been a more compelling sports image, outside an actual competition, than the horrific sight of Nancy Kerrigan crying out "Why me?" while sitting on the hallway floor after the unprecedented attack after her 1994 U.S. Nationals practice session. It still would have been a major story, but the presence of a video camera—at the moment when Kerrigan thought her lifelong dreams of Olympic success had just been stolen from her—assured that millions would suddenly pay added attention to the goings-on in figure skating.

And if one skater had some goons turn on one of her competitors, wouldn't it be likely that the entire activity is full of backbiting and ill wishes?

Well, to be truthful, no.

To spend any time with skaters and witness how they talk to one another over meals and in the halls on a tour such as *Champions on Ice* is to realize that the rivalries one has heard about are nothing but fabrications. As Guddat points out, although the skaters are competitive, "they're competitive on the ice. They want to put on their best performance. The competitions are healthy, and the skaters don't carry the competition backstage. Everybody has a good time. Everybody's friendly and everybody's joking."

But a TV commercial extolling the merits of skaters' being best friends wouldn't encourage many non-hard-core skating fans to watch skating on TV. That's why you'll often hear commercials using words that sound more like they're describing armed conflict among warring nations, such as the two slogans mentioned previously, the Battle of the Brians and the Duel of the Carmens.

After the 1994 Winter Olympics, the media, which had put Kerrigan in the limelight every day after the attack, seemed to do an about-face on the type of exposure she got. Everything she did and said was big news—except now the "big" news portrayed her in less than positive terms.

Kerrigan left the Olympics before the closing ceremony and flew to Disney World for a parade in her honor. She had decided that the past was past; now she had an opportunity to get on with her life and enjoy her business opportunities, in which Disney played a large role. On the float she was riding, the microphone picked up Kerrigan commenting, "This is the corniest thing I ever did." She wasn't criticizing Disney or the parade, and yet the comment was broadcast on all the networks. More small "big" news. According to Kerrigan, she never wore any of her medals once a competition's medal ceremony was over, since she had been taught when she was young "that to wear my medals would be showing off, as if saying, 'Everyone look at what I did.'" The comment that got sent around the world was in reference to being told to wear her medal on the float. The simple comment was broadcast on news programs and became the butt of jokes on a variety of talk shows.

Yet, despite their obsession with skaters' personal lives and the willingness to treat small, inconsequential comments and events as major stories, the media are the best friend figure skating has ever had. Through the media's efforts, millions who will never see a live skating competition or exhibition get a chance to enjoy the artistry and athleticism of one of the world's greatest and most remarkable sports.

Skaters as Rock Stars

Top-level figure skaters and rock stars do have a few things in common. Both are at the top of their profession and perform in large arenas in front of thousands of screaming fans. And both have trouble slipping out in public and enjoying some privacy when desired.

One of the problems skaters encounter in this age of media saturation is that, on occasion, fans get carried away with their enthusiasm. Usually this is innocent enough, sometimes involving fans' waiting outside arenas for autographs. Often skaters will pay their respects by going to the area where the fans are and signing a number of autographs before they have to move on to their hotel or next destination. The people who run the shows will sometimes create an area, cordoned off from the skaters, where fans can wait, hoping for their favorite skater to come by. If you've been to one of these post-performance sessions, you've heard all the screaming that happens when skaters walk out to sign autographs or just to say hi.

On rare occasions, skaters have felt threatened by someone who did not know where to draw the line. There was a famous stalking case in which a skater had to go to court to protect herself from a fan. When another skater hired a bodyguard in the early 1990s, supposedly to protect herself from rowdy fans, people scoffed. Today, though, the idea appears to have been ahead of its time.

Guddat has seen some fans display a lack of respect for certain skaters' personal spaces, stating that "some of the skaters have to look over their shoulders all the time." She's seen fans go up to skaters in restaurants to seek autographs, not really caring if the skater is trying to eat in peace or carry on a conversation. Guddat observes, "It's almost too hard for the skaters to go out and sign a few program books because other fans will . . . demand the skater also sign their book. They are really offended if the skaters don't spend an hour or two after the show signing autographs.

"Once they step off the ice, they're still as big a star as they are on the ice and every bit as much still in the spotlight. It's kind of getting to the point where they're being treated like rock stars."

Someday, perhaps, we'll talk about rock stars being treated like figure skaters.

part *Five*

An Armchair Guide

The Mystique of Judging

TO THOSE WHO AREN'T JUDGING SKATING PERFORmances, the art and science of judging often seem to make as much sense as the deepest mysteries of the universe. One is often left to ponder, "Why did they put that skater ahead of the other skater?" Or, one might think, "I could have done a better job in picking the right skater."

Yes, judges are human. They do make mistakes. And sometimes, though not as often as they used to be, they are victims of national bias. But, for the most part, they are ordinary people called upon to do a most out-of-the-ordinary thing—separate themselves from the emotions of the fans as they watch skaters going through their routines, intensely analyze every performance down to the smallest detail, and then give it a number.

Judges rate each skater based on the performance delivered at the time—they don't rank a skater order-wise with the other skaters. The scores of all the judges combined ultimately decide what the order will be. Well, sort of. Something called ordinals seems to confuse a majority of fans.

Figure skating is unique to the world of winter sports. In speed skating, downhill skiing, and cross-country skiing, the fastest performance wins the gold. In ski jumping, points for the distance jumped are combined with style points, the score given for how graceful the jump was. The athlete with the most points wins.

In figure skating, higher points are generally better than lower points, but only if they translate to lower ordinals. What ordinals mean is that the score a judge gives each skater is important only when compared with the scores the same judge gave to other skaters. Whoever receives the highest score from a given judge in a particular competition wins that judge's "card" with an ordinal of 1. But actual scores are irrelevant. All that matters on each judge's card is the placement order of each skater.

If two skaters tie score-wise, the lower ordinal would go to the one with the higher Presentation mark. (It used to be that the Technical Merit marks broke a tie, but the ISU decided that too much emphasis was being placed on jumps. This is how the tie between Oksana Baiul and Nancy Kerrigan was broken—in Baiul's favor—at the 1994 Winter Olympics.)

However, that's not all there is to ordinals. The skater with a *major-ity* of first-place ordinals will win that segment of the competition. The skater with a *majority* of second-place ordinals will be in second, and so on.

Sometimes a skater will see his position drop *two* placements after just *one* other score is announced, a score whose ordinals were not as good as what he had been awarded. It's possible that a single new score can turn everything upside down. It's all in how the ordinals compare, and not just *near* the end of the competition but at the very, very end.

This is why computers are used to figure out the ordinal rank-ings. In the days before computers and calculators, this was all done by hand. Imagine how time-consuming that must have been, because each new score could juggle the order, and every ordinal from every judge had to be factored in.

One more thing needs to be considered: After each stage of a competition, the placement of each skater is multiplied by a fac-tored value representing the percentage of the total represented by that stage of the competition. For example, in singles skating (and Pairs), the short program is worth one-third (33.3 percent) of the total score and the long program/free skate is worth two-thirds (66.7 percent). Each skater's placement after the short program is multiplied by a factored placement of .5. Their placement after the long program is multiplied by a factored placement of 1.0 (because two-thirds and 1.0 is twice what one-third and .5 is). At the end, the factored placements are added together for every skater. The skater with lowest factored placements wins.

If you still don't understand how the system works, don't worry. You're far from alone. This is why there is increased talk of eliminating the entire ordinal system, so that when one skater beats another skater, their position relative to each other won't change, no matter how the other skaters place.

Sometimes a judge will be suspended by the ISU for making a big mistake or for exhibiting obvious nationalism, purposely putting skaters from his own country above skaters of other countries when it is clearly wrong to do so. At other times, a judge might merely be reprimanded for his error, if the ISU feels he made an honest mistake. The incident mentioned earlier, about a Soviet judge "propping up" Alexandr Fadeev in 1986 by giving him marks of 5.8 and 5.9 while other judges scored him in the 5.4 to 5.6 range, resulted in a suspension for nationalistic bias.

Although they sit right next to the ice, judges don't always have the best seats from which to view a competition. Because they sit in a straight row along the side of the ice, the judge farthest away from where a skater is at the time may have difficulty seeing exactly what is happening. Sometimes a judge will miss a quick fall or bobble in its entirety because she happens to be looking down at her judge's sheet to mark something when the incident happens. And because judges don't have access to instant replay, they can't make up what they miss.

In the past, good but unknown skaters have sometimes skated quite well on the national or world level, but have not received good marks. Sometimes good well-known skaters have skated poorly and gotten very good scores, making it seem as if familiarity were a hidden criteria on the judging sheets.

* * *

What Judges Look For

Each year, the ISU provides all judges with a suggested list of deductions for maneuvers that are executed less than perfectly or are omitted altogether. In a recent competitive season, a jump, jump combination, flying spin, spin, or spin combination that was performed incorrectly would result in a deduction ranging from .1 to .4, the range allowing for the judge to deduct less for small bobbles and more for large ones. Total omission of the above maneuvers, if they were required elements in a singles short program, was a flat .5 deduction. It's rare for skaters to omit a move completely, the sequence of moves being so ingrained in their muscle memory. But when it happens, it's disastrous in the short program. (If skaters omit a move in the long program, they can try it again later on without penalty.)

There are other suggested deductions for other maneuvers, and Pairs have their own list of deductions and omissions. For example, among their list of deductions, a less-than-perfect lift, twist lift, solo jump, solo spin, pair spin combination, or death spiral would earn a deduction in the range of .1 to .4, while a total omission was a deduction of .5.

While fans respond to the drama of jumps and spins for single skaters and lifts and throws for Pairs, the judges have to analyze things the average fan doesn't pay much attention to—the quality of the maneuver, good technique, and the cleanness of the takeoff and landing, among other things. They must also take into consideration the difficulty of the maneuvers. A skater having problems on a simple maneuver is going to be scored lower than a skater having problems on extremely difficult maneuvers. For instance, a missed quad jump won't count off as much as a missed double jump. Falling on an easy jump, especially in the short program of required elements, can sound a death knell to a skater's hopes.

Judges carefully study stroking technique across the ice: Is the skater gliding gracefully or is she attacking the ice in an inappropriate fashion? They look for proper leg position in stroking and spins. Some world-level skaters still have problems with achieving proper leg positions because they weren't taught correctly from the beginning. Judges take into consideration the quality and variety of the skater's footwork: Is she employing several techniques, or does she do everything the same way? Do spins stay in one spot as they should, or does the skater "travel" down the ice while attempting to spin in one spot?

Much of judging is objective, based not on opinion but on fact. The maneuvers are either clean or they aren't. The jumps are hit or they're missed. But some elements of a skating performance can be judged only subjectively. This is where the Presentation marks come in. The judges ask themselves questions such as, How is the music interpreted? Is the music appropriate for the skater? Does the interpretation bring something unique to the music? Does the skater put her soul into the presentation? Does the judge feel a special connection between the skater and the music?

Skaters must be in great physical condition, certainly among the world's top athletes. But they must possess a further quality—one that can't be measured by muscle mass, aerobic conditioning, or flexibility. They must have in their soul the ability to interpret music and give it life on the rink. The goal of every skater, coach, and choreographer is to let the music dictate the action.

To score high, skaters have to make the judges "feel" their performance. Judges won't "feel" the performance if it doesn't have a sense of flow, if it feels chopped up. The entire routine must seem as if it has a beginning of anticipation, a middle of wonder, and an ending of awe. If jumps are just thrown in wherever they land, one after another, and it appears that the elements of the routine could be switched around any which way without affecting the continuity, then the skater has failed to create an appropriate sense of flow. But a good routine with good flow will give the impression that the elements are in the order they are because they couldn't possibly be in any other order. Everything is so right that to put something else in or take something out would be sacrilege.

A fall on a jump, while devastating to the Technical Merit marks, may not affect the Presentation marks at all, especially if the flow of the program isn't affected. However, if the skater interrupts the program or even skates around in a daze for a while after a hard fall, then the Presentation marks would be affected because the flow of the program was damaged.

When a skating performance flows from beginning to end, it turns into something far beyond a mere routine—it turns into a work of art.

Short and Long Programs

In the short program, singles and Pairs skate for no longer than two minutes and forty seconds. The judges' first mark is for Required Elements, and the second mark is for Presentation. The list of Required (technical) Elements each year is dictated by the ISU. For singles skaters, the list dictates which jumps, combination jumps, and footwork sequences (sometimes called "straight line sequence") are to be performed by all skaters, to the music of their choice. For Pairs skaters, the list specifies which jumps, spins, lifts, death spirals, and footwork sequences are to be performed. These elements are to be worked into the music in an artistic fashion.

Technical points are deducted for incorrectly performed elements, and any missed elements cannot be attempted later in the short program without a mandatory penalty, in contrast to the long program, where skaters are allowed to throw in another attempt at an element they missed earlier.

Ice Dancers don't have a short program. Instead, they start their part of the competition with a compulsory dance program, usually requiring them to skate two dances from specific styles that were assigned by the ISU before the season began, such as fox-trot, tango, blues, or flamenco. They receive two sets of marks, for Technique and for Timing/Expression. Then they move into the original dance phase, where they perform to music of their own choice to a specified style of dance. This program is only two minutes in length and is often referred to as the "original set pattern dance," as the skaters perform to a very specific dance pattern that they created themselves. Judges' marks are given for Composition and Presentation. Instead of a long program, Ice Dancers skate a free dance of four minutes in length and are judged on Technical Merit and Presentation, just like singles skaters and Pairs.

Compulsories count for 20 percent of the total score (10 percent for each compulsory dance), the original dance counts for 30 percent, and the free dance counts for the remaining 50 percent.

Curiously, the Men and Pairs have a free skate time limit of four and a half minutes, while the Ladies have to skate only for four minutes. The long program has fewer rules than the short program, with no required elements. Think of it as a blank canvas upon which the skaters are free to do whatever they wish. But if a skater doesn't perform the same feats as the other skaters, then he will receive a lower score. That's why whenever someone perfects a new, more difficult jump, all the other skaters feel obligated to put one in their repertoire as soon as possible.

Often, only a certain number of skaters will move on to the long program. In the long program, skaters are broken into groups of no more than six for singles and four for Pairs and Ice Dancing. The skaters then warm up on the ice with other skaters who are in their group.

Skaters draw for position within each group, with the lower-placing skaters from the short program taking the ice in the earlier groups and the higher-placing skaters taking the ice in the later groups. There has long been speculation on the value of skating last in the final group. Some feel that judges hold out on giving their highest possible score—even for what seems to be a perfect performance—to skaters who aren't on last, just in case the last skater comes out and delivers a performance that is even better. Judges want to have some "head room" to work with, which is gone if they give perfect scores out too early.

By having the skaters draw for position, everyone has an equal chance of skating last. Of course, judges will tell you that it makes no difference where someone skates—they'll get whatever score they deserve no matter what order they skate in. So, maybe the thought that it is better to be on last is a myth.

HOW TO RECOGNIZE SELECTED JUMPS, SPINS, AND PAIRS MOVES

JUMPS

Edge jumps *do not utilize the toe pick of the foot opposite to the takeoff foot to assist the jump.*

axel   an edge jump launched while moving forward, making it easy to identify. Requires an extra half rotation to land backward. (A double axel is really 2 ½ rotations; a triple is 3 ½.) Takeoff: forward outside edge. Landing: back outside edge of opposite foot.

loop   an edge jump launched while moving backward. Takeoff: back outside edge. Landing: back outside edge of same foot.

salchow   an edge jump launched while moving backward. Takeoff: back inside edge. Landing: back outside edge of opposite foot.

Toe jumps *utilize the toe pick of the foot opposite to the takeoff foot to assist the jump.*

flip   a toe jump launched while moving backward. Takeoff: back inside edge. Landing: back outside edge of opposite foot.

lutz   a toe jump launched while moving backward. The rotation is in the opposite direction of the broad curved approach. Takeoff: back outside edge. Landing: back outside edge of opposite foot.

toe loop   a toe jump launched while moving backward. Takeoff: back outside edge. Landing: back outside edge of same foot.

SPINS

camel   a variety of spins where the body and free leg typically remain parallel to the ice

combination   any number of spins combined with no stop in between. Feet and body positions are changed during the continuous spin, ideally with no loss of speed.

layback   a spin in which the back is arched, the head is tilted back, and the free foot is lifted behind the skater. The Biellmann Spin is a type of layback spin.

scratch   a spin in which the body is straight, with arms pulled in tightly for speed. When this is done quickly, the skater becomes a blur.

sit   a variety of spins where the body appears to be sitting while rotating, with the free leg extended in any number of positions

PAIRS MOVES

death spiral   The man spins in one place while holding the hand of the woman. She glides around him on one foot, with her back and head close to the ice.

hand-to-hand loop lift   The woman starts in front, facing the same direction as the man. He lifts her overhead, and she continues to face the same direction in a sitting position, supported by the man from below, with her hands behind her.

hydrant lift   The woman is thrown over the head of the man while he's skating backward. He turns half a rotation and catches the woman, who is now facing him.

lateral twist   The man throws the woman overhead. She rotates in the air and is caught by the man and set back on the ice.

platter lift   The man lifts the woman overhead with his hands on her hips. She remains parallel to the ice, facing his back.

split twist   The man throws the woman into the air. She goes into a split position before rotating vertically to the ice, and is caught by the man and set back on the ice.

star lift   The man lifts the woman overhead by her hips, from his side. Her legs are in a scissors position. One of her hands may touch his shoulder, or she may stay hands-free.

throw jump   The man assists the woman in becoming airborne. Before landing backward, she completes up to three revolutions. Common throw jumps include the throw double axel, throw triple salchow, and triple toe loop.

toe overhead lift The man lifts the woman overhead from his side, with assistance from her toe pick. She enters the overhead split position from behind his head, facing the same direction as he.

twist lift The man lifts the woman overhead while both are skating backward. She's tossed in the air and rotates any number of rotations before being caught by the man and set back on the ice.

The World Figure Skating Museum and Hall of Fame

THE WORLD FIGURE SKATING MUSEUM AND HALL OF FAME IS a not-for-profit facility dedicated to preserving figure skating's past and present, offering fans a glimpse into all aspects of the sport. The museum is located next to the United States Figure Skating Association's National Headquarters in Colorado Springs, Colorado.

Sponsored by the USFSA, the museum is recognized by the International Skating Union as the official repository of the history and records of figure skating. It also contains the World Figure Skating Hall of Fame and the United States Figure Skating Hall of Fame.

The museum contains the world's largest collection of figure skating art and memorabilia, and skating artifacts from the past four centuries. The collection of historical documents and reference materials from skating's earliest days includes insights on the personalities that made skating what it is, as well as films and videos of skating performances. There is also a large collection of skating costumes, skates, medals, trophies, photos, posters, show programs, magazines, and collectors' pins.

The museum is located at 20 First Street, Colorado Springs, CO 80906. For more information, phone 719-635-5200. On the Internet, the museum's Web page can be found at http://www.worldskatingmuseum.org.

USFSA

The United States Figure Skating Association (USFSA) is the national governing body of amateur skating in the United States. It was founded in 1921 with only seven charter member clubs; there are now about five hundred skate club members and about 125,000 individual members, consisting of athletes and supporters. Membership more than doubled in the ten years prior to 1998. The USFSA is a member of both the International Skating Union and the United States Olympic Committee. About 1,250 events are sanctioned by the USFSA each year.

Skating Magazine is the official publication of the USFSA. In-depth articles include a look at various skating personalities as well as articles on health and fitness. Ticket information and schedules for USFSA events are a regular feature, as are extensive results of various regional, national, and world competitions.

Each year, the USFSA distributes several hundred thousand dollars in athlete grants and assistance programs to members of the United States World Team as well as to juvenile-level skaters. The USFSA also processes at least five thousand skill tests per month, administered to skaters throughout the country so that the skaters can move up to the next level of proficiency.

The USFSA maintains the USFSA Memorial Fund, offering financial assistance to skaters in need. The fund was founded in memory of those who perished in the 1961 airplane crash on the way to the World Championships.

Sports science is an increasingly important part of USFSA activity. At the USFSA Sports Science and Medicine Camp, skaters are educated about how to enhance their athletic performance and prevent injuries. They learn about sports medicine, warm-up techniques, psychology, nutrition, biomechanics, exercise physiology, strength training, and conditioning.

The USFSA's National Headquarters is at 20 First Street, Colorado Springs, CO 80906. For more information, phone 719-635-5200 or send e-mail to USFSA1@aol.com. USFSA Online can be accessed through America Online. Keyword: USFSA. On the Internet, look for the USFSA home page at http://www.usfsa.org.

CFSA

Figure skating is one of the oldest sports in Canada and a national pastime. Reflecting this, the Canadian Figure Skating Association (CFSA, known to French-speaking Canadians as Association canadienne de patinage artistique) is the largest figure skating governing body in the world. The national governing body of amateur figure skating in Canada has more than 190,000 members and at least 1,465 member clubs.

The CFSA is a member of the International Skating Union and selects the Canadian World and Olympic figure skating teams, with approval from the Canadian Olympic Association.

Approximately 74 percent of CFSA members are registered in recreational skating programs, and 17 percent actively take CFSA tests to move up to higher levels of competition—these test skaters average fourteen years of age. The CFSA offers a variety of skating programs for skaters from preschool age through adulthood, as well as testing programs on a variety of levels.

The CFSA distributes funding to approximately one thousand athletes each year. Athlete Trust Grants are available to the top eight novice, junior, and senior entrants at the Canadian Championships. In addition, the CFSA provides standards, training, and certification for coaches and judges.

The CFSA's National Office is located at 1600 James Naismith Drive, Gloucester, Ontario K1B 5N4, Canada. A mail order department provides publications, jewelry, music, and other items of interest. For more information, phone 613-748-5635, or access the Internet home page at http://www.cfsa.ca.

American Skating World

The first issue of *American Skating World* was published in 1981, promoting figure skating at a time when the mass media had not yet discovered the sport to any great degree. Since then, this monthly, year-round, independent publication has brought fans closer to the action of figure skating, taking them behind the scenes with articles about all major competitions, exhibitions, and tours.

Reviews are offered of the latest skating books, videos, and skating tours. A number of interviews are presented each month with top skaters, as well as those not yet in the limelight. Regular features look at the inside workings of judging and the latest developments in health and fitness. Other regular features include classified ads, an extensive list of upcoming skating events throughout the world, and a listing of skating events to be televised.

American Skating World also annually presents the World Professional Skater of the Year award.

American Skating World is located at 1816 Brownsville Road, Pittsburgh, PA 15210-3908. For more information, phone 800-245-6280. Outside the United States, call 412-885-7600. For subscription information, you may also send an e-mail to subscription@americansk8world.com. Or, visit its Web page at http://www.americansk8world.com.

Other Web Pages

1. International Skating Union
   http://virtserve.interhop.net/~isu
2. United States Olympic Committee
   http://www.olympic-usa.org
3. Champions on Ice
   http://www.championsonice.com/index.html
4. Stars on Ice
   http://www.starsonice.com

OLYMPIC AND WORLD FIGURE SKATING CHAMPIONS

WORLD FIGURE SKATING CHAMPIONS

Men/Ladies/Pairs/Ice Dancing

1896	Gilbert Fuchs, Germany
1897	Gustav Hugel, Austria
1898	Henning Grenander, Sweden
1899	Gustav Hugel, Austria
1900	Gustav Hugel, Austria
1901	Ulrich Salchow, Sweden
1902	Ulrich Salchow, Sweden
1903	Ulrich Salchow, Sweden
1904	Ulrich Salchow, Sweden
1905	Ulrich Salchow, Sweden
1906	Gilbert Fuchs, Germany
	Madge Syers, Great Britain
1907	Ulrich Salchow, Sweden
	Madge Syers, Great Britain
1908	Ulrich Salchow, Sweden
	Lily Kronberger, Hungary
	Anna Hubler and Heinrich Burger, Germany
1909	Ulrich Salchow, Sweden
	Lily Kronberger, Hungary
	Phyllis Johnson and James Johnson, Great Britain
1910	Ulrich Salchow, Sweden
	Lily Kronberger, Hungary
	Anna Hubler and Heinrich Burger, Germany
1911	Ulrich Salchow, Sweden
	Lily Kronberger, Hungary
	Ludowika Eilers and Walter Jakobsson, Finland
1912	Fritz Kachler, Austria
	Opika von Horvath, Hungary
	Phyllis Johnson and James Johnson, Great Britain
1913	Fritz Kachler, Austria
	Opika von Horvath, Hungary
	Helene Engelmann and Karl Mejstrik, Austria
1914	Gosta Sandahl, Sweden
	Opika von Horvath, Hungary
	Ludowika Jakobsson and Walter Jakobsson, Finland
1915–1921	No championship held (World War I)
1922	Gillis Grafstrom, Sweden
	Herma Plank-Szabo, Austria
	Helene Engelmann and Alfred Berger, Austria
1923	Fritz Kachler, Austria
	Herma Plank-Szabo, Austria
	Ludowika Jakobsson and Walter Jakobsson, Finland
1924	Gillis Grafstrom, Sweden
	Herma Plank-Szabo, Austria
	Helene Engelmann and Alfred Berger, Austria
1925	Willy Boeckl, Austria
	Herma Plank-Szabo, Austria
	Herma Jaross-Szabo and Ludwig Wrede, Austria
1926	Willy Boeckl, Austria
	Herma Jaross-Szabo, Austria
	Andrée Joly and Pierre Brunet, France
1927	Willy Boeckl, Austria
	Sonja Henie, Norway
	Herma Jaross-Szabo and Ludwig Wrede, Austria
1928	Willy Boeckl, Austria
	Sonja Henie, Norway
	Andrée Joly and Pierre Brunet, France
1929	Gillis Grafstrom, Sweden
	Sonja Henie, Norway
	Lilly Scholz and Otto Kaiser, Austria
1930	Karl Schafer, Austria
	Sonja Henie, Norway
	Andrée Joly and Pierre Brunet, France
1931	Karl Schafer, Austria
	Sonja Henie, Norway
	Emilie Rotter and Laszlo Szollas, Hungary

1932   Karl Schafer, Austria
Sonja Henie, Norway
Andrée Joly and Pierre Brunet,
France

1933   Karl Schafer, Austria
Sonja Henie, Norway
Emilie Rotter and Laszlo Szollas,
Hungary

1934   Karl Schafer, Austria
Sonja Henie, Norway
Emilie Rotter and Laszlo Szollas,
Hungary

1935   Karl Schafer, Austria
Sonja Henie, Norway
Emilie Rotter and Laszlo Szollas,
Hungary

1936   Karl Schafer, Austria
Sonja Henie, Norway
Maxi Herber and Ernst Baier,
Germany

1937   Felix Kaspar, Austria
Cecilia Colledge, Great Britain
Maxi Herber and Ernst Baier,
Germany

1938   Felix Kaspar, Austria
Megan Taylor, Great Britain
Maxi Herber and Ernst Baier,
Germany

1939   Graham Sharp, Great Britain
Megan Taylor, Great Britain
Maxi Herber and Ernst Baier,
Germany

1940–1946 No championship held (World War II)

Note: Prior to 1940, the Men's, Ladies', and
Pairs World Championships were often held in
different cities.

1947   **Stockholm, Sweden**
Hans Gerschwiler, Switzerland
Barbara Ann Scott, Canada
Micheline Lannoy and Pierre
Baugniet, Belgium

1948   **Davos, Switzerland**
Richard Button, U.S.A.
Barbara Ann Scott, Canada

Micheline Lannoy and Pierre
Baugniet, Belgium

1949   **Paris, France**
Richard Button, U.S.A.
Alena Vrzanova, Czechoslovakia
Andrea Kekesy and Ede Kiraly,
Hungary

1950   **London, Great Britain**
Richard Button, U.S.A.
Alena Vrzanova, Czechoslovakia
Karol Kennedy and Peter Kennedy,
U.S.A.

1951   **Milan, Italy**
Richard Button, U.S.A.
Jeannette Altwegg, Great Britain
Ria Falk and Paul Falk, Federal
Republic of Germany

1952   **Paris, France** (first year for Ice
Dancing)
Richard Button, U.S.A.
Jacqueline du Bief, France
Ria Falk and Paul Falk, Federal
Republic of Germany
Jean Westwood and Lawrence
Demmy, Great Britain

1953   **Davos, Switzerland**
Hayes A. Jenkins, U.S.A.
Tenley Albright, U.S.A.
Jennifer Nicks and John Nicks,
Great Britain
Jean Westwood and Lawrence
Demmy, Great Britain

1954   **Oslo, Norway**
Hayes A. Jenkins, U.S.A.
Gundi Busch, Federal Republic of
Germany
Frances Dafoe and Norris Bowden,
Canada
Jean Westwood and Lawrence
Demmy, Great Britain

1955   **Vienna, Austria**
Hayes A. Jenkins, U.S.A.
Tenley Albright, U.S.A.
Frances Dafoe and Norris Bowden,
Canada

Jean Westwood and Lawrence
Demmy, Great Britain

1956 **Garmisch, Federal Republic of
Germany**
Hayes A. Jenkins, U.S.A.
Carol Heiss, U.S.A.
Elizabeth Schwarz and Kurt Oppelt,
Austria
Pamela Weight and Paul Thomas,
Great Britain

1957 **Colorado Springs, U.S.A.**
David Jenkins, U.S.A.
Carol Heiss, U.S.A.
Barbara Wagner and Robert Paul,
Canada
June Markham and Courtney Jones,
Great Britain

1958 **Paris, France**
David Jenkins, U.S.A.
Carol Heiss, U.S.A.
Barbara Wagner and Robert Paul,
Canada
June Markham and Courtney Jones,
Great Britain

1959 **Colorado Springs, U.S.A.**
David Jenkins, U.S.A.
Carol Heiss, U.S.A.
Barbara Wagner and Robert Paul,
Canada
Doreen Denny and Courtney Jones,
Great Britain

1960 **Vancouver, Canada**
Alain Giletti, France
Carol Heiss, U.S.A.
Barbara Wagner and Robert Paul,
Canada
Doreen Denny and Courtney Jones,
Great Britain

1961 No championship held (U.S.A.
World Team plane crash)

1962 **Prague, Czechoslovakia**
Donald Jackson, Canada
Sjoukje Dijkstra, Holland
Maria Jelinek and Otto Jelinek,
Canada

Eva Romanova and Pavel Roman,
Czechoslovakia

1963 **Cortina, Italy**
Donald McPherson, Canada
Sjoukje Dijkstra, Holland
Marika Kilius and Hans Baumler,
Federal Republic of Germany
Eva Romanova and Pavel Roman,
Czechoslovakia

1964 **Dortmund, Federal Republic of
Germany**
Manfred Schnelldorfer, Federal
Republic of Germany
Sjoukje Dijkstra, Holland
Marika Kilius and Hans Baumler,
Federal Republic of Germany
Eva Romanova and Pavel Roman,
Czechoslovakia

1965 **Colorado Springs, U.S.A.**
Alain Calmat, France
Petra Burka, Canada
Ludmila Belousova and Oleg
Protopopov, U.S.S.R.
Eva Romanova and Pavel Roman,
Czechoslovakia

1966 **Davos, Switzerland**
Emmerich Danzer, Austria
Peggy Fleming, U.S.A.
Ludmila Belousova and Oleg
Protopopov, U.S.S.R.
Diane Towler and Bernard Ford,
Great Britain

1967 **Vienna, Austria**
Emmerich Danzer, Austria
Peggy Fleming, U.S.A.
Ludmila Belousova and Oleg
Protopopov, U.S.S.R.
Diane Towler and Bernard Ford,
Great Britain

1968 **Geneva, Switzerland**
Emmerich Danzer, Austria
Peggy Fleming, U.S.A.
Ludmila Belousova and Oleg
Protopopov, U.S.S.R.
Diane Towler and Bernard Ford,

Great Britain

1969 **Colorado Springs, U.S.A.**
Tim Wood, U.S.A.
Gabriele Seyfert, German
Democratic Republic
Irina Rodnina and Alexsei Ulanov,
U.S.S.R.
Diane Towler and Bernard Ford,
Great Britain

1970 **Ljubljana, Yugoslavia**
Tim Wood, U.S.A.
Gabriele Seyfert, German
Democratic Republic
Irina Rodnina and Alexsei Ulanov,
U.S.S.R.
Liudmila Pakhomova and Aleksandr
Gorshkov, U.S.S.R.

1971 **Lyons, France**
Ondrej Nepela, Czechoslovakia
Beatrix Schuba, Austria
Irina Rodnina and Alexsei Ulanov,
U.S.S.R.
Liudmila Pakhomova and Aleksandr
Gorshkov, U.S.S.R.

1972 **Calgary, Canada**
Ondrej Nepela, Czechoslovakia
Beatrix Schuba, Austria
Irina Rodnina and Alexsei Ulanov,
U.S.S.R.
Liudmila Pakhomova and Aleksandr
Gorshkov, U.S.S.R.

1973 **Bratislava, Czechoslovakia**
Ondrej Nepela, Czechoslovakia
Karen Magnussen, Canada
Irina Rodnina and Alexandr Zaitsev,
U.S.S.R.
Liudmila Pakhomova and Aleksandr
Gorshkov, U.S.S.R.

1974 **Munich, Federal Republic of
Germany**
Jan Hoffmann, German Democratic
Republic
Christine Errath, German
Democratic Republic
Irina Rodnina and Alexandr Zaitsev,

U.S.S.R.
Liudmila Pakhomova and Aleksandr
Gorshkov, U.S.S.R.

1975 **Colorado Springs, U.S.A.**
Sergei Volkov, U.S.S.R.
Dianne de Leeuw, Holland
Irina Rodnina and Alexandr Zaitsev,
U.S.S.R.
Irina Moiseeva and Andrei
Minenkov, U.S.S.R.

1976 **Gothenberg, Sweden**
John Curry, Great Britain
Dorothy Hamill, U.S.A.
Irina Rodnina and Alexandr Zaitsev,
U.S.S.R.
Liudmila Pakhomova and Aleksandr
Gorshkov, U.S.S.R.

1977 **Tokyo, Japan**
Vladimir Kovalev, U.S.S.R.
Linda Fratianne, U.S.A.
Irina Rodnina and Alexandr Zaitsev,
U.S.S.R.
Irina Moiseeva and Andrei
Minenkov, U.S.S.R.

1978 **Ottawa, Canada**
Charles Tickner, U.S.A.
Anett Pötzsch, German Democratic
Republic
Irina Rodnina and Alexandr Zaitsev,
U.S.S.R.
Natalia Linichuk and Gennadi
Karponosov, U.S.S.R.

1979 **Vienna, Austria**
Vladimir Kovalev, U.S.S.R.
Linda Fratianne, U.S.A.
Tai Babilonia and Randy Gardner,
U.S.A.
Natalia Linichuk and Gennadi
Karponosov, U.S.S.R.

1980 **Dortmund, Federal Republic of
Germany**
Jan Hoffmann, German Democratic
Republic
Anett Pötzsch, German Democratic
Republic

Marina Cherkasova and Sergei
  Shakhrai, U.S.S.R.
Krisztina Regoeczy and Andras
  Sallay, Hungary
1981　**Hartford, U.S.A.**
Scott Hamilton, U.S.A.
Denise Biellmann, Switzerland
Irina Vorobieva and Igor Lisovsky,
  U.S.S.R.
Jayne Torvill and Christopher Dean,
  Great Britain
1982　**Copenhagen, Denmark**
Scott Hamilton, U.S.A.
Elaine Zayak, U.S.A.
Sabine Baess and Tassilo Thierbach,
  German Democratic Republic
Jayne Torvill and Christopher Dean,
  Great Britain
1983　**Helsinki, Finland**
Scott Hamilton, U.S.A.
Rosalynn Sumners, U.S.A.
Elena Valova and Oleg Vasiliev,
  U.S.S.R.
Jayne Torvill and Christopher Dean,
  Great Britain
1984　**Ottawa, Canada**
Scott Hamilton, U.S.A.
Katarina Witt, German Democratic
  Republic
Barbara Underhill and Paul Martini,
  Canada
Jayne Torvill and Christopher Dean,
  Great Britain
1985　**Tokyo, Japan**
Alexandr Fadeev, U.S.S.R.
Katarina Witt, German Democratic
  Republic
Elena Valova and Oleg Vasiliev,
  U.S.S.R.
Natalia Bestemianova and Andrei
  Bukin, U.S.S.R.
1986　**Geneva, Switzerland**
Brian Boitano, U.S.A.
Debi Thomas, U.S.A.
Ekaterina Gordeeva and Sergei

Grinkov, U.S.S.R.
Natalia Bestemianova and Andrei
  Bukin, U.S.S.R.
1987　**Cincinnati, U.S.A.**
Brian Orser, Canada
Katarina Witt, German Democratic
  Republic
Ekaterina Gordeeva and Sergei
  Grinkov, U.S.S.R.
Natalia Bestemianova and Andrei
  Bukin, U.S.S.R.
1988　**Budapest, Hungary**
Brian Boitano, U.S.A.
Katarina Witt, German Democratic
  Republic
Elena Valova and Oleg Vasiliev,
  U.S.S.R.
Natalia Bestemianova and Andrei
  Bukin, U.S.S.R.
1989　**Paris, France**
Kurt Browning, Canada
Midori Ito, Japan
Ekaterina Gordeeva and Sergei
  Grinkov, U.S.S.R.
Marina Klimova and Sergei
  Ponomarenko, U.S.S.R.
1990　**Halifax, Canada**
Kurt Browning, Canada
Jill Trenary, U.S.A.
Ekaterina Gordeeva and Sergei
  Grinkov, U.S.S.R.
Marina Klimova and Sergei
  Ponomarenko, U.S.S.R.
1991　**Munich, Germany**
Kurt Browning, Canada
Kristi Yamaguchi, U.S.A.
Natalia Mishkutenok and Artur
  Dmitriev, U.S.S.R.
Isabelle Duchesnay and Paul
  Duchesnay, France
1992　**Oakland, U.S.A.**
Viktor Petrenko, Commonwealth of
  Independent States
Kristi Yamaguchi, U.S.A.
Natalia Mishkutenok and Artur

Dmitriev, Commonwealth of
Independent States

Marina Klimova and Sergei
Ponomarenko, Commonwealth
of Independent States

1993   **Prague, Czechoslovakia**
Kurt Browning, Canada
Oksana Baiul, Ukraine
Isabelle Brasseur and Lloyd Eisler,
Canada
Maia Usova and Alexandr Zhulin,
Russia

1994   **Chiba, Japan**
Elvis Stojko, Canada
Yuka Sato, Japan
Evgenia Shishkova and Vadim
Naumov, Russia
Oksana Grishuk and Evgeny Platov,
Russia

1995   **Birmingham, Great Britain**
Elvis Stojko, Canada
Lu Chen, China
Radka Kovarikova and Rene
Novotny, Czechoslovakia
Oksana Grishuk and Evgeny Platov,
Russia

1996   **Edmonton, Canada**
Todd Eldredge, U.S.A.
Michelle Kwan, U.S.A.
Evgenia Shishkova and Vadim
Naumov, Russia
Oksana Grishuk and Evgeny Platov,
Russia

1997   **Lausanne, Switzerland**
Elvis Stojko, Canada
Tara Lipinski, U.S.A.
Mandy Wötzel and Ingo Steuer,
Germany
Oksana Grishuk and Evgeny Platov,
Russia

1998   **Minneapolis, U.S.A.**
Alexei Yagudin, Russia
Michelle Kwan, U.S.A.
Elena Berezhnaya and Anton
Sikharulidze, Russia

Anjelika Krylova and Oleg
Ovsyannikov, Russia

**WINTER OLYMPIC FIGURE SKATING
CHAMPIONS**

Men/Ladies/Pairs/Ice Dancing

1908   **London, Great Britain**
Ulrich Salchow, Sweden
Madge Syers, Great Britain
Anna Hubler and Heinrich Burger,
Germany

1912   No skating events held

1916   No Olympic Games held

1920   **Antwerp, Belgium**
Gillis Grafstrom, Sweden
Magda Julin-Mauroy, Sweden
Ludowika Jakobsson and Walter
Jakobsson, Finland

1924   **Chamonix, France**
Gillis Grafstrom, Sweden
Herma Plank-Szabo, Austria
Helene Engelmann and Alfred
Berger, Austria

1928   **St. Moritz, Switzerland**
Gillis Grafstrom, Sweden
Sonja Henie, Norway
Andrée Joly and Pierre Brunet,
France

1932   **Lake Placid, U.S.A.**
Karl Schafer, Austria
Sonja Henie, Norway
Andrée Joly and Pierre Brunet,
France

1936   **Garmisch, Germany**
Karl Schafer, Austria
Sonja Henie, Norway
Maxi Herber and Ernst Baier,
Germany

1940, 1944   No Olympic Games held

1948   **St. Moritz, Switzerland**
Richard Button, U.S.A.
Barbara Ann Scott, Canada
Micheline Lannoy and Pierre
Baugniet, Belgium

1952   **Oslo, Norway**
Richard Button, U.S.A.
Jeannette Altwegg, Great Britain
Ria Falk and Paul Falk, Federal
Republic of Germany

1956   **Cortina, Italy**
Hayes A. Jenkins, U.S.A.
Tenley Albright, U.S.A.
Elizabeth Schwarz and Kurt Oppelt,
Austria

1960   **Squaw Valley, U.S.A.**
David Jenkins, U.S.A.
Carol Heiss, U.S.A.
Barbara Wagner and Robert Paul,
Canada

1964   **Innsbruck, Austria**
Manfred Schnelldorfer, Federal
Republic of Germany
Sjoukje Dijkstra, Holland
Ludmila Belousova and Oleg
Protopopov, U.S.S.R.

1968   **Grenoble, France**
Wolfgang Schwarz, Austria
Peggy Fleming, U.S.A.
Ludmila Belousova and Oleg
Protopopov, U.S.S.R.

1972   **Sapporo, Japan**
Ondrej Nepela, Czechoslovakia
Beatrix Schuba, Austria
Irina Rodnina and Alexsei Ulanov,
U.S.S.R.

1976   **Innsbruck, Austria** (first year for
Ice Dancing)
John Curry, Great Britain
Dorothy Hamill, U.S.A.
Irina Rodnina and Alexandr Zaitsev,
U.S.S.R.
Liudmila Pakhomova and Aleksandr
Gorshkov, U.S.S.R.

1980   **Lake Placid, U.S.A.**
Robin Cousins, Great Britain
Anett Pötzsch, German Democratic
Republic
Irina Rodnina and Alexandr Zaitsev,
U.S.S.R.

Natalia Linichuk and Gennadi
Karponosov, U.S.S.R.

1984   **Sarajevo, Yugoslavia**
Scott Hamilton, U.S.A.
Katarina Witt, German Democratic
Republic
Elena Valova and Oleg Vasiliev,
U.S.S.R.
Jayne Torvill and Christopher Dean,
Great Britain

1988   **Calgary, Canada**
Brian Boitano, U.S.A.
Katarina Witt, German Democratic
Republic
Ekaterina Gordeeva and Sergei
Grinkov, U.S.S.R.
Natalia Bestemianova and Andrei
Bukin, U.S.S.R.

1992   **Albertville, France**
Viktor Petrenko, Commonwealth of
Independent States
Kristi Yamaguchi, U.S.A.
Natalia Mishkutenok and Artur
Dmitriev, Commonwealth of
Independent States
Marina Klimova and Sergei
Ponomarenko, Commonwealth
of Independent States

1994   **Lillehammer, Norway**
Alexei Urmanov, Russia
Oksana Baiul, Ukraine
Ekaterina Gordeeva and Sergei
Grinkov, Russia
Oksana Grishuk and Evgeny Platov,
Russia

1998   **Nagano, Japan**
Ilia Kulik, Russia
Tara Lipinski, U.S.A.
Oksana Kazakova and Artur
Dmitriev, Russia
Pasha Grishuk and Evgeny Platov,
Russia